What
Genera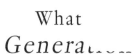

When I read the first chapters of *Generation to Generation*, my first thought was, "This inspires me to be a better father!" As I read more, I became convinced that I could *actually become* a better father and grandfather. Bishop Richard Hilton doesn't beat us over the head with guilt for failing to be a great dad or mom; instead, he ignites optimism and excitement of how we can shape our legacies as parents—and not just as physical parents, but also as fathers and mothers in the faith. Today, I'm more encouraged to pass on the faith and the baton of leadership than before I read this book. More than mere concepts, you'll find pragmatic suggestions and inspiring stories so you can be the parent you've always wanted to be. Read and be transformed.

—Dr. Samuel R. Chand, Leadership Consultant and author
of *Cracking Your Church's Culture Code* (www.samchand.com)

Richard Hilton has been my friend and my Pastor since I was twenty-five years old, and today some thirty years later, he remains the same. I connected with him because, even as a young man, he had all the attributes of a good father: he's kind, strong, knowledgeable and teachable. In his book you will get the benefit of the grace that is on his life. As you read it, you will understand why it has never crossed my mind to leave his side. You will read about what a son learns from a father and what a father leaves for sons and daughters, and you will realize why I feel so blessed to call Bishop Hilton my pastor.
Read *Generation to Generation* and discover the value—and the values—of true fathers and the blessing received by those, like myself, who have been privileged to know one.

—B. Courtney McBath, D. Min., Senior Founding Pastor of
Calvary Revival Church, Norfolk, Virginia (Bcourtneymcbath.org)

This book is of vital importance for those of us who desire to leave a legacy of positive influence for the generations to follow. The real-life stories are riveting, and the insights are revelatory. Every mentor or parent *needs* this book!

—Brian C. Greene, Senior Pastor, Pentecostal Tabernacle, Cambridge, Massachusetts, International Bishop, United Pentecostal Council of the Assemblies of God, Inc.

When I was growing up, I was lucky enough to have the best father and Pastor, my "Papa Bear." He was a daily example of love, commitment and steadfastness in his role as a father and Pastor. That's why I know this book is a must-read for any leader and spiritual father in the faith, as well as natural fathers. In addition, *Generation to Generation* is an invaluable resource for those going through transition and succession.

—Rick Hilton, Minister of Music at Calvary Church, Johnson City, Tennessee

My sweet Daddy has been a shining example of how to be an effective spiritual father to thousands—as well as an exemplary natural father to my brothers and me. In a time when absentee fathers abound, his life and integrity point directly to the Cross of Calvary and emphasize the importance of relationships. He is my very first love, my all-time favorite super-hero, my biggest supporter, and my very first glimpse of Jesus! Although I've had to share him with the world because of his God-given ability to father the fatherless, I am his one and only girl! My amazing Dad's love for his family and his love for the church have inspired me to run passionately after my Jesus and respond to the grace of God's calling to ministry.

—Rebecca Davis, Operations Manager, Washington County Economic Development Council

GENERATION

to

GENERATION

Developing *faithful* young leaders
in the home & *church*

Richard L. Hilton

DREAM
RELEASER
ENTERPRISES

*To the best friend and person I've ever known,
my wife, Theresa. Thanks for serving our
generation and the next by the will of God!*

Acts 13:36

CONTENTS

ACKNOWLEDGEMENTS

My life is the product of the loving and powerful influences of many people. I particularly want to thank a number of people:

To my father, Harry Robert Hilton, who beat the odds! Dad, you survived the Great Depression, endured a troubled childhood, beat alcoholism, and overcame the scars of war to become an amazing father. I miss you!

To my mother, Anna Lee Hilton. Your prayer life and steadfast love for Jesus, Dad, and your children taught me the meaning of commitment!

To my spiritual father, Dr. B. J. Pruitt. Thank you for giving yourself to the Lord and to me. You impacted four generations of my family for Christ: my parents, my wife and me, my children, and my grandchildren!

To my children, Robbie and Monica, Ricky and Erica, and Rebecca and Jesse. You are everything I ever dreamed of!

Lastly, to my grandchildren, Chloe, Judah, Aaliyah, Oliver, Andrew, Addison, Levi, Colin, Ava, and Ryan. Thanks for the smiles, laughter, and motivation to finish strong and leave a legacy.

FOREWORD

Usually, the person writing the foreword for a book is some kind of celebrity. I'm an exception. When my dad asked me to write the foreword for his book, I was humbled and thrilled. I'm not a great author, I'm not a famous and powerful business leader, and I'm certainly not a celebrity—unless you ask my son Judah. He thinks I could have played in the NBA and won *American Idol*. I'm just a son who has the most wonderful life because I've been loved by an exceptional father and mother.

Was my childhood perfect? No. It was far better than that. It was *full!* Full of hugs, spankings, heartbreaks, victories, fights, and kisses. Sometimes, that all happened in one day! Were my parents perfect? No. They were better than that. They were *real*. Really loving, gentle, forgiving, quick to say, "I'm sorry," loyal, and godly. This isn't a book about how to be a *perfect* father. This is a book about how to be a *real* father . . . like my Dad.

Every morning of my childhood, my father sang to us before we went to school:

"Get up, get out of bed.

Drag a comb across your head.

Brush your teeth and take a shower.

It is, it is, the getting up hour.

Get up, get up, get up, get out of bed."

As I grow older, the thing I appreciate the most about my Dad is his investment of time. He took time to teach me how to tie my shoes, ride my bike, hit a baseball, shoot a basketball, and so much more. More than anything, I remember that he was there—with me and for me. I can't recall everything he said in all those moments together, but the fact that he was there made his words powerful. He was *in the moment*, not distracted by his own goals that had nothing to do with his family or lost in some television show. My Dad gave me a most precious commodity: his time. It's the most valuable thing we have, and you can't buy more of it. When I think about my Dad, the clearest picture in my mind isn't him preaching. It's him sitting at our kitchen table with his Bible, a devotional, and a book he was reading. With his pen in hand and a heart on fire, he was spending time with Jesus.

I know this book will help you because the man who wrote it has been with Jesus.

In October of 2013, I was given the privilege to become the Lead Pastor of the church my Dad planted almost 30 years ago when he was just 29. On Easter Sunday the following year, I preached to the largest crowds our church has ever seen. That day, I imagined my dad 30 years earlier, in jeans and a button up short sleeve shirt pulling weeds and mowing the lawn at our tiny church building in Elizabethton. As I spoke that Easter morning, I realized I was standing on a platform of influence my dad had built. And that day, I was preaching in front of a young man, my son, who is already a better man than me. Whether he becomes a pastor, a plumber, a painter, or a paleontologist, he will have received a legacy from my dad passed down through me.

—Robbie Hilton

Lead Pastor, Calvary Church of the Tri-Cities

CHAPTER ONE

GENERATIONS

"I write not these things to shame you, but as my beloved sons I warn you. For though ye have ten thousand instructors in Christ, yet have ye not many fathers: for in Christ Jesus I have begotten you through the gospel. Wherefore I beseech you, be ye followers of me" (1 Corinthians 4:14-16 KJV).

Every generation has suffered from a serious shortage of fathers. It was a problem in the days of the Apostle Paul in Palestine and the Roman Empire, and it continues to be a dilemma today in a very different culture. This isn't just a crisis in our secular society; it's also a problem within Christianity. Paul's words are indeed true: "you do not have many fathers."

Being a father is one of the most challenging and the most rewarding roles a man can fulfill. Loving, responsive children bring the highest measure of fulfillment to life. If men could see the incredible pride in a child's eyes in being a valued son or daughter, all men would want to be a dad!

As the father of three wonderful children and the grandfather of ten amazing grandchildren, I have personally experienced the joy of children and the super-sized joy of grandchildren. Listen to these words of King Solomon: "Children's children are a crown to the aged, and parents are the pride of their children" (Proverbs 17:6).

FATHERS: ANCIENT AND MODERN

Today, many parents have a very distorted view of their kids. Some see their sons and daughters as ways to live out their own dreams, so they put enormous pressure on their children to succeed in sports, academics, dance, or some other pursuit. Others see their children as nuisances. These parents are absorbed in their own goals, and they resent every moment their kids pull them away from their self-indulgent pursuits. And of course, an alarming number of children never see their first bright day of life. The tragedy of abortion cuts their lives short. In whatever way a child is devalued, overlooked, or neglected, everyone loses. The child, of course, misses the warmth and instruction of attentive, loving parents. And the parents and grandparents miss the joy of seeing a little life blossom into maturity.

God has put it in the heart of parents to instinctively treasure their children. This is why Abraham wouldn't give up hope for a child, even when he was 99 years old. God had promised him a son, and through that child, Abraham would become the father of many nations (Genesis 12:1-3 and Romans 4:17-18). When the promised son was born, Abraham named him "Isaac," which means "joy and laughter." When the baby came, joy came! Did you know that this is the first time the word "love" is used in the Bible? It is in reference to Abraham's love for his son Isaac (Genesis 22:2). If Isaac hadn't been born, several nations (especially Israel) wouldn't exist today—and an old man wouldn't have had the supreme joy of seeing God fulfill His promise as he watched his little boy grow up.

Being a father is a huge blessing. In fact, they are multiplied because they're shared blessings: shared fulfillment, shared dreams, a shared history, and a shared legacy. Children turn smiles into laughter! Just one hug from a grandchild brings comfort in middle of life's deepest sorrows. And when life comes to an end—and it will—we won't be alone at death. Those we love will be around us. When God promised Jacob that

Being a father is a huge blessing. In fact, they are multiplied because they're shared blessings: shared fulfillment, shared dreams, a shared history, and a shared legacy.

he would become a great nation, He also promised that he would not be alone when he died. God showed him that his son, Joseph, would be at his side and that Joseph would close his father's eyes in death: "and Joseph will put his hands upon your eyes" (Genesis 46:1-4). As the hour of death neared, all of Jacob's sons and grandchildren gathered around him. Jacob blessed them, and their presence blessed Jacob.

I've had a "Jacob and Joseph" experience, and I'll treasure it until my last breath. Our family was together when my father, Harry Robert Hilton, passed away. We gathered in his hospital room in the Intensive Care Unit. My mother, Anna, was holding Daddy's hand as he gazed into the loving eyes of his children and our spouses, along with several grandchildren. Unable to speak, Dad looked around the room at each of us. Catching our eyes, he smiled at us individually. We were very sad, but our sadness was filled with genuine hope and love. We sang an old gospel song:

"Master, Redeemer, Savior of the world.

Wonderful, Counselor, bright morning star.

Lily of the valley, provider, and friend.

He was yesterday. He will be tomorrow.

The beginning and end."

As we sang, Daddy turned his gaze toward Momma, the love of his life. Then, as a single tear fell from his eye and rolled down his cheek, he smiled at her and closed his eyes in death.

I miss him to this very day. No one can take the place of my father. I've had many instructors, mentors, and teachers—but only one father. It has been 10 years since he died, yet every day my Dad becomes more and more "the pride of *his* children" (Proverbs 17:6 NLT). Every day I think of my Dad and recall some wonderful memory. Others may have taught me more, but Dad did more to fill my heart and shape my character. He left me his passion for preaching, his love for Christ Jesus, and his compassion for the hurting and helpless. He gave me what none other could...his freckles, his big smile, his funny laugh, his slumped shoulders, and his crooked nose.

Today, our culture is broken. The roles of father, mother, husband, and wife are confused. Marriage is compromised, fidelity is a lost art, and family is becoming an archaic term. Some may have no reference point or understanding of the role of fathers because their own fathers were absent or abusive. Yet there's still a father-shaped vacuum in their hearts because God the Father put it there (Genesis 2:24).

Sometimes, the story of a family takes some odd twists and turns. I know. I've experienced a shock or two.

A SURPRISE BROTHER

My father volunteered for military service when he was only 16 years old. Like many in his generation, he had a deep love for America, even though he had faced severe hardships growing up in the Great Depression. After World War II, Dad served in the Occupation of Japan and in Korea. While in Japan, he met a lovely girl from the Philippines named Josephine. Dad fell in love. He affectionately called her "Josie." Josie spoke Japanese and served the U.S. military as a translator. They married in Japan and soon had a little boy they named Terry Lee. When the Korean War flared up, Dad was sent into combat on the peninsula. The fighting was intense, but the news about casualties was sometimes wrong. Military authorities reported to Josie that Dad had been killed in action. After grieving his death, Josie remarried and left Japan.

In fact, Dad had been severely wounded, but he survived by the grace of God. After Dad's recovery, he couldn't find Josie. He returned to America. He met my mother in Tennessee and together raised our family. Although Dad couldn't find out what happened to Josie and Terry, he continually prayed that God would reunite him with his son. Every holiday, Dad solemnly prayed with our family for Terry.

Finally, just six years ago, Terry and I found each other! Terry was 57 and I was 52. I was amazed…Terry looks so much like our father! When we met face-to-face, I instantly realized Terry has Dad's smile, his expressions, his walk, and his compassion for the less fortunate and children. The similarities are amazing. Terry is such a treasure. Thank God, I have my big brother!

But Terry missed meeting Dad. Dad had passed away less than two years before we found each other. Terry and his wife, Janet, flew from California to Tennessee and stayed in our home for two weeks. He was filled with questions about Dad. I did my best to describe his laugh, likes and dislikes, favorite foods, personality, passions, and purpose. Terry wanted to learn all he could about our father. To discover more about Dad, he spent time with my mother, Anna. Terry also visited Dad's brother, Wayne, and his newfound younger siblings, David, Patti, Carol, and me. Terry wanted to see Dad's hometown, his childhood home—and his grave. At the grave, Terry spent several hours alone. Every evening we looked at our family albums of photographs, his and mine. We laughed, we talked, we embraced—and we cried.

Terry Lee was grateful to meet all of us and spend time with his brothers, sisters, and our Mom, but he still missed Dad. Although

Terry never met Dad, he loved him! In the same way, we loved Terry, even before we ever met him. His longing for a relationship with Dad still breaks my heart. Terry is a wonderful man, a community leader, and has accomplished so much. Yet there was always a longing—a cry for his father.

Terry's not alone. All of us cry out for our fathers. In our pursuit, we uncover more love and heartache than we ever imagined, and in the quest, we may find three things we thought we'd never find: ourselves, our purpose, and God. In this book, we'll look at the importance of fathers in the life of an individual, a family, a community of faith, and a society. We'll draw strongly on the principles the Apostle Paul outlines in his relationship with Timothy, his "spiritual son" in the faith. But these principles are applied in three distinct ways: as a father raises his own children, as spiritual parents mentor spiritual sons and daughters, and as all parents instill faith, hope, love, and purpose in their children. In other words, virtually all of us have a role in the lives of young people, so all of us can learn from Paul's example.

> **In our pursuit, we uncover more love and heartache than we ever imagined, and in the quest, we may find three things we thought we'd never find: ourselves, our purpose, and God.**

Before we get to Paul's principles, I want to describe the conditions of our present culture and tell the story about the parents who have shaped my life.

CHAPTER TWO

FINDING A FATHER

"A father to the fatherless, a defender of widows, is
God in his holy dwelling" (Psalm 68:5).

Many *absentee* fathers know who their children are, yet they aren't around them to show the love and support their kids desperately need. Other difficult dads aren't absent at all—they're *abusive*. Their anger boils over at those who are most vulnerable. Most fathers aren't on the far extremes of pathological, destructive behavior. They try their best to be good fathers, but they're discouraged because they fail so often. All dads need instruction concerning fatherhood, but we need even more than instruction—we need to see real, living examples of genuine, godly fathers because many men will never witness the love of a father any other way! The Apostle Paul spoke of the need of every generation for more than instruction: "you might have ten thousand instructors in Christ, yet you do not have many fathers" (1 Corinthians 4:15A NKJ).

All good parents teach, train, and instruct their children, but the desperate need of the heart is greater than academic lessons can supply. The things I miss most about my Dad are relational, not instructional. I miss our talks, his reassuring hand on my shoulder, his embrace, his prayers at holidays … I miss his presence. We learn much more by sharing life than sharing a lesson plan. We learn more about life in the living room than the classroom. The solution for America's problems isn't in the White House or the schoolhouse. The answers are found in your house and my house!

The family is crucial, but it's under attack. The creation of strong, stable, nurturing, inspiring families is the plan of God to change a city, a culture, even a nation. Before there were governments, written languages, communities, cities, nations, or even churches, God instituted the family! God has always cared for the fatherless and the widow: "A father of the fatherless, a defender of widows, is

God in His holy habitation. God sets the solitary in families" (Psalm 68:5-6a NKJ). God doesn't want anyone to be alone. God Himself is a Father! God loves the family. In fact, family is God's big idea!

As God was creating the heavens and the earth, each day ended with the statement: "and God saw that it was good" (Genesis 1), but when God made Adam, He said, "It is not good that the man should be alone; I will make him an help meet for him" (Genesis 2:18 KJV). In response, God made Eve and brought her to Adam. Right then and there, God performed the first wedding (Genesis 2:21-25). Both God and Adam liked the idea. They delighted in each other. Soon, they heard the pitter-patter of little feet, and the first family began to grow! Of course, blessing families was God's plan all along (Genesis 1:27-28; 12:3B).

MY DAD

My father and my brother Terry had much in common. Both had a longing for a relationship with their birth fathers. I've had the joy of telling Dad's story for Terry's eager ears. As I told it, I learned even more about our father. Dad was born May 28th, 1930 to Joseph Robert Hilton ("Joe Bob") and Nellie Sawyers. Joe Bob was a moonshiner and a gambler. His rough life contributed to his death when he was only 52 years old. The children's exposure to the "family business" and the harshness of the Great Depression eventually led to many of Joe Bob's children doing their best to simply survive.

When Dad was 7 years old, a man named Speedy Pruitt found him sleeping in a refrigerator box in an alley in Elizabethton, Tennessee. Speedy took Dad to his home where his wife, Annie, fed Dad many meals during the lean years of the Depression. Because of the Pruitt's kindness, my father not only survived; he developed lifelong friendships with their family. In many ways, they became his family, and Speedy revealed the love of a father to my Dad. The Pruitts showed Dad the affection, strength, and warmth of a close-knit family. His experiences with them were influential in my Dad coming to know Christ years later.

In the absence of men as good role models in the home today, we need more "spiritual fathers and mothers" like Speedy and Annie. Dr. B. J. Pruitt (Bobby Jack Pruitt), one of Speedy's sons and one of my father's best boyhood friends, has been this kind of father to me. Dr. Pruitt became my spiritual father and has meant the world to me. The connection to the Pruitt family continues to this day, three generations later, in the lives of my children and grandchildren! When they saw that little boy in the refrigerator box many decades ago, Speedy and Annie Pruitt could not have known the impact they would have on generations to come.

The Apostle Paul did more than simply teach about the necessity of fathers; he became a father to many spiritual sons. He took upon himself the responsibility of establishing relationships, mentoring, and developing the lives of several young men. One of them was a man named Timothy. In his letters, Paul referred to him as "Timothy, my own son in the faith" (1 Timothy 1:2 KJV). Like Paul, our generation must take the responsibility of preparing

> **When they saw that little boy in the refrigerator box many decades ago, Speedy and Annie Pruitt could not have known the impact they would have on generations to come.**

the next generation to fulfill their destiny. In this book, we'll use the relationship of Paul with Timothy to illustrate the quality and depth of the connection men can have with their own children—and that men can have with other kids who need a father figure.

MY MOM

When Paul met Timothy, the young man wasn't fatherless. However, Timothy's birth father had little or no spiritual impact upon the young man's life. It seems that his father either wasn't around or simply wasn't involved in his life. But Timothy wasn't abandoned. He was deeply influenced by his mother Eunice and his grandmother Lois. They taught him the Scriptures, and more importantly, they imparted a great faith in God (2 Timothy 1:5; 3:15). Like many children today, Timothy had a wonderful example of faith in his mother and grandmother. Thank God for faithful women!

My mother, Anna Hilton, is like Eunice and Lois. She's an amazing Christian woman—she's a prayer warrior with a servant's heart. She loved my Dad and lived for Jesus. She loved and served him even when my father was losing his battle with PTSD, heart disease, and multiple strokes. What a woman!

In 1972, I gave my heart and life to Christ—I was radically saved during what became known as "The Jesus Movement." I was a long-haired hippie who knew he was called to preach, but my long hair and bell-bottomed jeans posed a threat to many legalistic believers in the '70s. After I'd become the Youth Pastor of a church in Tennessee, our youth group traveled to sing at a church in North Carolina. When the pastor and deacons saw my long hair, they were alarmed. I guess they assumed my appearance would be a bad influence on the young people of their church. Their solution was to forbid me to come inside. They made me stay on the bus while the rest of my youth group shared in the church. I felt hurt, and it confused many of the students in our ministry.

When church leaders focus on the outward appearance, they miss the meaning of the gospel message—and young people notice. Many leave and don't come back to church! In spite of the way I was treated, I stayed strong in faith because my mother believed in me and encouraged me to pursue the call of God upon my life—in spite of the criticism. I wouldn't be where I am today without her prayers, her love, and her support.

My mother is still living and works in her local church. She is 76; after her grandson died, she adopted her great granddaughter and is raising her to serve Jesus. Thank God for faithful mothers! It's these kind of women God uses as spiritual mothers in His kingdom.

DR. PRUITT

My story was a little like Timothy's—we both had great mothers. And like Timothy, God brought a good and godly father in the faith into my life as well. Finding a spiritual father isn't as hard as it seems. First, you have to identify those around you that already have a strong spiritual influence in your life. Second, you distinguish between the "ten thousand instructors" and discover who has "begotten you through the gospel." That is, who is the person who loves you and whose faith you can trust enough to follow (1 Corinthians 4:15-17). It may not be the same person who led you to Christ, but it's the person who influences your growth and challenges you to fulfill your God-given destiny.

Dr. B. J. Pruitt was a church planter who established the first Bible College that I attended. I grew up hearing of his faith. When I met him and heard him speak, I was deeply influenced by his passion for missions. In fact, he took me on my very first mission trip. He led my wife's mother to the Lord, and he baptized both of them. From my vantage point, it wasn't difficult to see who God placed as a spiritual father in my life! I'm so grateful to God for him. Dr. Pruitt was to me what Paul was to Timothy. In 1974, he opened his heart to this hippie preacher, and his signature is on my ordination certificate on May 1st, 1976. I've completed my fourth decade of ministry, and Dr. Pruitt has faithfully counseled me every step of the way.

Dr. Pruitt is now almost 83 years old, and he's still preaching! He continues to speak into my life, and he mentors many others whom he considers his "own sons in the faith" (1 Timothy 1:2).

I'm convinced that every young man needs a "father in the faith," and every young woman needs a "spiritual mother." Each of us should have at least three pivotal relationships. First, we need friends in our generation—peers who challenge us, comfort us, and encourage us. Second, we should have those we are teaching and discipling the next generation. And third, we need spiritual fathers from the previous generation who are guiding us forward.

> I'm convinced that every young man needs a "father in the faith," and every young woman needs a "spiritual mother."

GENERATION TO GENERATION

Transition and succession are two unique processes. *Transition* is the process that takes place when a father passes on faith, values, history, and purpose to the next generation. *Succession* takes place when a father has successfully completed that process and is ready to pass the baton. The psalmist reported, "Let each generation tell its children of your mighty acts" (Psalm 145:4 NLT).

I often hear fathers say of their sons, "He isn't ready for the transition." That's a misplaced assumption. When children are born, the transition begins! Transition is getting them ready for succession. Transition is happening as the little child learns to walk and talk, develops life disciplines as a child, chooses friends, uncovers talents, and finds a destiny worth living for. Succession, though, can happen in a single day—and it often does! Unexpected death or tragedy has prematurely thrust many into leadership roles. So, fathers need to be about the task of transition! A good definition of transition is: "training for the position." Don't wait for them to grow up, grow them up! It's never too early to start, and it's never to late to begin.

If high school seniors aren't ready for graduation, whose fault is that? If our sons in the faith aren't ready to assume leadership, who's responsible? My successor at our church was ready four or five years before we implemented our succession. The problem was that I wasn't ready to let go of the baton!

The truth is, we hardly ever think the next generation is ready. I know I wasn't ready for full-time evangelism when I was 19, or my first pastorate when I was 22, or church planting at 29. There are some lessons we can only learn "on the job"! I definitely know I wasn't ready for marriage and children! Don't forget the grace given to us when we began. Don't wait too long to release the next generation.

The good metaphor of transition and succession is running a relay race. With one hand we reach back to receive the baton from the previous generation who has helped us reach our destiny. And with the other hand, we're stretching the baton forward to the out-stretched, waiting hand of the next generation.

Stop making excuses, and stop justifying your reluctance. If your children aren't ready to take leadership of their lives, focus your time and attention on training them. Give them enough resources to give them confidence, but push them enough to challenge them. And then watch as they fly! Celebrate when they pass you by. That's your role as a father, leader, and mentor to the next generation!

Give them enough resources to give them confidence, but push them enough to challenge them. And then watch as they fly!

But your role isn't finished. Keep running after you pass the baton. You must keep the pace because the next generation is picking up the pace. Don't stop running. There are more young people who need your help. They're waiting for someone to train them and pass the baton to them, too. And don't pass the waiting generation by holding on to the baton too long.

CHAPTER THREE

THE ROOM OF MY FATHER

"And the Lord hath performed his word that he spake, and I am risen up in the room of David my father" (1 Kings 8:20a KJV).

P erhaps the most dramatic and sacred ceremonies of all time occurred at the dedication of Solomon's Temple. Untold riches were spent in the building of that majestic house of worship! Solomon's father, David, had left incredibly beautiful and valuable "things" (1Kings 7:51) for his son to use in the decorations, including the blueprints for the construction and approximately $1.5 to 2 billion dollars in silver and gold (1Chronicles 29:1-9)! Solomon was very grateful to his father. He mentioned David at least eight times in his prayer of dedication. Solomon confessed that he was fulfilling his father's deepest dreams by building the Temple. Obviously, the wishes of his father were paramount to Solomon. After all, he had "risen up in the room of" his father.

The Hebrew word for "room" means: "beneath or below; instead of; or in lieu of." Solomon is saying, "I have risen up from beneath my father to take his place." Like Solomon, every child continues in the room his or her father built!

Solomon grew up in at least four rooms his father David had built:

The first room was *relationships.*

Solomon had the same enemies and the same friends as David. The first three years of Solomon's reign was a bloody transition. Solomon had to fight battles at home against enemies David had fought but hadn't defeated. While David was often victorious over the enemies attacking his kingdom, he was notoriously weak at home! David left Solomon some strained relationships that David should have resolved in his lifetime (1 Kings 2:5-9).

As fathers, we need to guard our relationships for the sake of our children. They are impacted by our relationship choices! At our church, as the time of transition was nearing the end and the time of succession drew close, I intentionally made necessary relationship adjustments in my staff and the ministry. I didn't want to leave behind any unfinished relational business!

The second room David built was *generosity.*

David was a giver. He loved the house of God and gave sacrificially to see that it was built. Solomon finished building the Temple so that he might honor the Lord and his father (1 Kings 8:17-20). Solomon grew up in the room of generosity built by his father. King David left the nation debt-free and at peace! We would do well to do the same for the next generation.

The third room is *worship.*

David was called "the sweet psalmist of Israel" because of his heart to worship God. David played the harp skillfully and composed music (2 Samuel 23:1 KJV). Solomon was like his dad in his love for worship. A little-known fact about Solomon is that he wrote 1,005 songs of worship (1 Kings 4:32). In addition, Solomon wrote a beautiful, romantic musical we know as "The Song of Solomon." Our worship must be fervent and sincere, because as we worship, we're building a room for our children!

Some fathers don't understand what it means to worship at home. I'm not talking about a choir

> Fathers can lead their families in worship by reading a passage from the Bible, taking the initiative to pray, and talk about what God is doing in each person's life.

robes, an organ, and a pulpit. Fathers can lead their families in worship by reading a passage from the Bible, taking the initiative to pray, and talk about what God is doing in each person's life. It may seem awkward at first, but don't miss this opportunity to point your wife and your children to the Lord! You'll get used to leading in this way, and you'll love it.

The fourth room is *weaknesses.*

David was a he-man with a she-weakness. In spite of David's love for God, he had multiple wives and committed adultery. David's affair was with Bathsheba, the mother of Solomon. For him, I'm sure that sitting around the dinner table with his siblings and his father's six wives made for some interesting family conversations! By the time he was an adult, Solomon was growing up in his father's room of weakness. While his father David had six wives, Solomon had seven hundred—and 300 more concubines! (1 Kings 11:1-3)

Solomon's experience teaches us two important father/son principles.

1. Children rise in the rooms their father builds.

Solomon himself admonishes us: "Enter not into the path of the wicked, and go not in the way of evil men" (Proverbs 4:14 KJV). That's great advice, but it's tough for children to obey since they're born into the path their parents are walking! I've heard it said, "What we allow in moderation, our children will excuse in excess." Let's be careful to build the right rooms!

2. Children will expand the dreams in their father's heart.

In the Scriptures, we see a clear progression: Joshua finished the tasks that had been given to his father in the faith, Moses, to conquer and inhabit the Promised Land (Joshua 11:15). Solomon finished David's dream of the Temple in Jerusalem. And Jesus provides the greatest example: He finished the work His Father had given Him to do (John 14:12). Let's be sure to leave a room filled with good dreams!

MY FATHER'S THINGS

Our father's things are very important to us. In fact, they're extremely valuable. And their impact has even more value in our eyes when our dads pass away. My Dad passed away nearly 10 years ago. Now, everything of his holds special value to me! Dad didn't have any material wealth to leave his children, but my mother gathered four priceless things from my father's room: a red paisley shirt with missing buttons, a broken watch, a box of rocks he had collected, and his military medals from World War II and the Korean Conflict.

While my inheritance may be insignificant to many people, it's priceless to me. Each of them reminds me of just how blessed I was to have a father, and they reveal so much of the life lessons Dad taught me. Far more than those tangible possessions, my father left me some things of infinite value. All fathers can leave these things to their kids.

First, *fathers leave power.*

Dad's red paisley shirt reminds me of God's anointing on his life. Anointing is simply, "God putting His super on your natural!" My father believed in the miraculous. I think of Elijah leaving his cloak for Elisha. Elijah's anointing, a double portion, came on Elisha, his son in the faith, the very day Elijah left this world for Heaven (2 Kings 2:9-13). Elisha went on to perform twice as many miracles as Elijah. Not long after my father was saved, he became an evangelist. Dad traveled preaching revivals and praying for the sick in the late 50's and early 60's. From local churches to tent meetings, our family traveled with Dad. Not only did we witness the miraculous in his ministry, we also experienced miracles in our family. My little brother David was born with leukemia. Later, his 7 year-old body was frail, weak, and dying. One night in an old-fashioned tent meeting in Johnson City, Tennessee in 1965, God completely healed him. Not only did my brother live; he thrived. Now, he has grandchildren of his own!

Jesus revealed the heart of Father God when He promised to leave the disciples with power to do what He had commissioned them to do (Luke 24:49; Acts 1:8-9). Dad's red paisley shirt reminds me that being a father means so much more than leaving material blessings. It involves leaving a faith that lets a child know that God can and will empower you to do what He calls you to do.

Second, *fathers leave purpose!*

Dad left me a broken watch. My father's watch speaks to me of purpose, dreams, and destiny. Jesus rejoiced in finishing the purpose His Father had given Him (John 17:4). My father had dreams that centered around two major desires: to build a church and to help the poor, especially children. Some think Dad failed to accomplish his dreams, but I respectfully disagree! God gave my father a dream, and He gave me a vision to fulfill that dream (Joel 2:28). When Dad walked in the last sanctuary we built before his death, he said, "This is the church I saw in my dream!" But that's not all. Dad had been hungry and homeless as a child. God has enabled us to feed the hungry and provide shelter for the homeless in our region. We also helped plant children's homes in both hemispheres!

Time is brief in duration and swift in its passing! Like Dad's watch, one day my heart will stop ticking, too. My Dad's lifetime passed by so swiftly. He often shared with me the number of dreams still in his heart, but he "ran out of time." My father's dreams were larger than his lifetime. I keep Dad's broken watch on my nightstand as a gentle reminder at the dawn of each new day to grab life by the throat and squeeze every ounce out of each second I'm alive—to enjoy my wife, children, and grandchildren (Ecclesiastes 9:9-10). Time is a gift from God. The wise man invests his strength and his time in his family. All too quickly our children grow up, leave home, and we're grandparents. My father's broken watch reminds me that being a father means prioritizing time with family. It's the relationship built by time spent together that leaves God-sized dreams in the heart of your children!

Third, *fathers leave prayer.*

Dad left me a box of rocks! My father loved to collect rocks that had unusual shapes and colors. After he prayed over them, he would seek out people in need of a miracle who were going through a difficult time. Dad would approach them, give them one of these rocks and say: "Whenever your faith is shaken, remember that Jesus is the Rock. He loves you, and I'm praying for you!" Dad believed in the power of prayer (Matthew 16:18-19). Some people thought Dad was a little too spiritual, but at Dad's funeral (we called it a "Home-going"), dozens of people told me that they had received miracles after Dad prayed for them. After hearing the stories, a lot of people want those rocks now, but I'm hanging on to them! They remind me of my heritage of prayer. My parents held prayer meetings in our home. In my heart, I can still hear the loud audible prayers of a dozen or more people praying in our living room when I was a child.

My mother kept a private place of prayer in every home where we lived. I'll never forget her praying for my salvation, weeping and saying, "O mighty God, save my son, Richard!"

Share your faith stories with your family. Keep a journal and write down the answers to your prayers. My father's box of rocks says that being a father means leaving a heritage of prayer.

Last, *fathers leave planted seed.*

The fourth of my father's things that I received was his military medals. The shadowbox of medals reminds me of his courage and patriotism. He was willing to sacrifice his life. My father's wounds in Korea prove his sacrificial heart of patriotism for our country, and he was willing to make sacrifices in other areas of his life as well. For instance, he was a sacrificial giver. Daddy loved to give and often gave his last dollar in an offering at church to help those in need. Dad and Mom were hospitable. They welcomed traveling preachers and needy families into our home. When I wasn't tall enough to see over the dinner table, I would sneak to the bottom of the stairs and listen to the late night stories that missionaries, preachers, and evangelists shared with my parents.

My family is still receiving the fruit from seeds my parents sowed! As I look at my children, I see the fruit of generations of love, honor, courage, faith, and gratitude. And I expect the seeds to produce even more fruit in the coming generations. The greatest hindrance to a harvest is the failure to sow the seed (Galatians 6:7). God the Father is the greatest example of sacrifice and courage (John 3:16). A father leaves planted seeds.

Sowing is a continual process. We're always planting seeds—good ones or bad ones. We are planting something in the soil of our children's hearts every day! My father's medals remind me that being a father requires planting seeds of courageous self-sacrifice that will result in a continual harvest being reaped in the lives of our children (Hebrews 7:9-10).

WHAT ARE YOU LEAVING?

All of us leave some things behind when we die. We hope we've planted seeds of character, integrity, faith, honesty, and loyalty. Being a father means that I take the responsibility of building an inheritance to leave behind. The inheritance is the responsibility of the parent, not the children (2 Corinthians 12:14). Like my father, you may not have wealth, but you can leave an incredibly valuable inheritance. You may not leave riches, but you can leave the legacy of faith, hope, and love! The story of our lives is much more than photographs scrolling on a video monitor in the funeral home. Our story lives on in the heart and memories of our children. My father's smile lives on in mine. I see his face in my mirror. Dad's faith is being revealed in the lives of his grandchildren. His dreams are still being fulfilled in his great grandchildren!

It's important that we realize the lasting impact of our lives on others. God always takes the long view of things. God the Father thinks in multiple generations, not just until lunch! Because God is a Father, He gives an inheritance to His children (Colossians 3:24). And when the Father makes promises, He extends them to succeeding generations. For instance, God identified Himself as the God of Abraham, Isaac, and Jacob, and He extended His covenant to their descendants (Exodus 2:24).

The Bible compares a life of faith to a mighty cedar tree. Your life provides shelter for the smaller fir trees that grow beneath your branches. As time passes, your life casts a larger shadow and has increasing influence. However, if you fall, you bring destruction on all who grow in the shade of your branches (Zechariah 11:1-2)!

What are you leaving behind?

CHAPTER FOUR

MEETING A FATHER

"But I trust in the Lord Jesus to send Timotheus shortly … for I have no man like minded, who will naturally care for your state. For all seek their own, not the things which are Jesus Christ's" (Philippians 2:19-21 KJV).

Sometimes, going to church is fairly uneventful, but occasionally, something dramatic happens there. One Sunday, my life took a major turn. I met a lovely young lady named Theresa Dawn Pritchard. She played the piano for worship and had the most beautiful voice I'd ever heard. More than that, she had the sweetest smile and was as pure as the fresh, wind-driven snow! She was—and still is—the best Christian I've ever known. As soon as I met her, I realized Theresa loved Jesus with all her heart. She made me want to be a good man.

I knew she was too young to ask her out for a date. She was only 15, and I was 20. I wasn't even thinking about dating. In fact, no one in our church was allowed to date back then. The culture and practice was very different from today. The old Southern custom was called "courting." My responsibility was to go to her father's house, tell him my intentions were noble, and then visit the whole family. As a matter of fact, I had to wait until her father approved the visits. After being allowed to visit, it was my responsibility to build a relationship with the family. Our customs also required me to ask her father if we could be married—before I asked Theresa!

Theresa's father had quite a reputation. He was the "John Wayne" of our hometown. Local legend said that Nathan Pritchard had never lost a fistfight. In addition, he was an accomplished quick-draw artist with a pistol. He spoke with a deep bass voice that struck fear into the heart of any would-be suitor ... had there been one so foolish to pursue Mr. Prichard's daughter! My own Pastor warned me, "Don't go courting Theresa. Her father will shoot you off the porch!" In spite of the warning, I went.

I'll never forget that warm summer day as long as I live. Before I went to the house, I rehearsed the words over and over until I could say them in a single breath. I knew that one breath might be all I had! I practiced the words as I drove to her house: "Mr. Pritchard, I'm Richard Hilton and I've come to court your daughter, Theresa. Mr. Pritchard, I'm Richard Hilton and I've come to court your daughter, Theresa."

I parked in the gravel driveway and walked up on the porch. As I knocked on the door, my hands trembled and my knees weakened. As I looked through the screen door, I could see him coming. He was even bigger than I had imagined! Suddenly, he stood on the other side of the screen door—dark eyes, dark black wavy hair and mustache, barrel chest and huge arms.

I nearly hyperventilated as I quickly screeched out loud the words I'd rehearsed. He waited for what seemed like days as I kept melting in front of him. Finally, he spoke with that deep voice, "Come on in." He turned and motioned for me to follow him into the house. I opened the screen door and walked behind him into their dining room. He led me to a tall gun cabinet. He opened the door, took a rifle in his hand and said, "This is a Winchester 30/30. I can shoot a hair off an ant's back at 100 yards. I'll use this on you if you lay a hand on my little girl!"

Realizing I was still alive, I stammered, "Mmmmmister Ppppritchard, I, I, I, I wwwould nnnever dddo that!" And I didn't! I kept my hands to myself through our courtship. I'd like to think it was because I was a gentleman. However, it just might have had a little to do with a certain threat uttered by Theresa's father! (I didn't fully understand Theresa's Dad until I became a father myself. Then, his stern warning made perfect sense.)

Theresa and I waited until her parents set a time they felt was right for us to marry. As a matter of fact, Theresa's mother and father selected the exact day. We married June 3rd, 1977. Then, 15 months after we married, on September 20th, 1978, we became the parents of a boy, Nathan Robert Hilton. Yes, he's named after Theresa's Dad. I know which side my bread's buttered on! We called him Robbie.

When Theresa and I courted and were married, her father wasn't a Christian. Her mother, Bobbie Jo, gave her heart to Christ in 1960, the year Theresa was born. Theresa said she grew up in "a well balanced home," praying on one end and cussing on the other! All kidding aside, I learned many important lessons about being a father from Theresa's unsaved Dad. When I met Nathan Prichard, I met a real father.

TRUE FATHERS

When you meet a true father, you observe three primary things.

First, *he gives*; *he's a provider*.

Nathan was one of the hardest working men I've ever known. He worked to provide for his family. When a person comes to know God as their Father, they meet a Provider. One of the names God is identified by on the Old Testament is "Jehovah-Jireh." It simply means, "God is my Provider" (Genesis 22:14 KJV). The Apostle Paul teaches, "The children ought not to lay up for the parents, but the parents for the children" (2 Corinthians 12:14-15 KJV). Unfortunately, some fathers aren't willing to take on the responsibility to provide for their own children. When the Apostle Paul checked on the state of the church at Philippi, he had a difficult time finding someone who would care for them "naturally" like a father would (Philippians 2:20), but Paul cared for them. True fathers like Paul are rare. When you meet a real father, you meet a provider! A father makes sure his children don't live in need, fear, or anxiety (Matthew 6:31-32). If you have a spiritual father, he will want to meet your needs before his own are met. He won't be "burdensome" to you (2 Corinthians 12:13).

Second, *he guards; he's a protector.*

As the rifle and the warning showed me, Theresa's father was the defender of his home. No one dared mess with him or his family. When Nathan was 60 years old, he knocked out a man 30 years his junior with one punch because the man had cursed his son. At that time, Nathan had been a Christian for only a few weeks, and he told me: "I'm sorry I knocked the young man out. I asked the Lord to forgive me, so promise me you won't tell Theresa." Well, who was I to argue with John Wayne? The point is that a father is the protector of his home. Our Heavenly Father promises to protect His children.

A true spiritual father will also have the same motive as our Heavenly Father. He would never expose you to the adversary by his words or his actions. He's a protector.

"No weapon formed against" God's child can "prosper." This protection is "the heritage" of all of God's children (Isaiah 54:17). A true spiritual father will also have the same motive as our Heavenly Father. He would never expose you to the adversary by his words or his actions. He's a protector. He can keep a confidence!

Last, *he guides; he gives purpose.*

God has a plan for every child. We are born with a future and a hope in the mind of our Heavenly Father (Jeremiah 29:11). Nathan taught his sons his trade. He raised them with the skills to succeed. My wife is a talented and gifted musician and songwriter. Even though Nathan had no musical talent, he taught himself to play the guitar and a little on the piano. Theresa's mother played piano, too. Nathan bought a huge upright piano, and their home was filled with music! As a father, it's our responsibility to "train up our children in the way they should go" (Proverbs 22:6 KJV). The original language is a picture of aiming an arrow at the bull's eye! Our children are "as arrows in the hand of a mighty man." One day they'll reach their target and will fill their father's heart with joy (Psalm 127:4-5 KJV). Spiritual fathers promote their sons and daughters. They receive more joy in the success of their children than in their own (3 John 4).

When my son Robbie was born, I became a father. Being a Dad brings overwhelming emotions. Those emotions overlap and toss the heart back and forth like a playground swing! Incredible joy is pushed out by the awe of responsibility. I still remember my scattered thoughts in those first moments holding my son. I can remember thinking, "He looks like my Dad . . . no, maybe he looks like Theresa's Mom." Then, turning on a dime, my next thoughts were: "Oh my God, how are we going to feed him? Maybe I could sell our car and get a cheaper one. How often does he eat? What do diapers cost anyway? Is he still breathing? Why is his head so pointy? We could move in with our parents. Did he just smile at me? Bet I could get a second job. Wow! I've got some growing up to do!" If you're a father, you can relate to my conflicting emotions and directions!

I knew being a father was a task I would have to grow into. I had no options. I instantly loved my son, even before I saw his face. So, ready or not, I had a son, and I was determined to become a loving, providing, protecting father! My heart's desire was to provide, to protect, and to give him purpose! More than three years later, our second child was born, Ricky. And then, finally, over two years later, God blessed us with a little girl, Rebecca.

CHILDREN AND MINISTRY

For our family, the early years were filled with physical hardships. We traveled from church to church as youth evangelists for nearly five years. Living out of a suitcase was difficult, but we made great memories and lifelong friendships. Then, in 1985, we planted a church in East Tennessee. For a time, we lived in the church, but the hardships aren't what Theresa and I remember. Actually, those early years produced some of our best memories. Theresa filled our days with love and laughter. No matter how poor we were, she never complained. Somehow, she made life a blast, and she turned a Sunday school room into a home. (Last year we were laughing about those early days, and it dawned on us

> The greatest gift parents can give their children is to joyfully love one another.

that we were homeless for several years—but we didn't know it! We were having too much fun to notice.)

The greatest gift parents can give their children is to joyfully love one another. The wisest thing a father can do is to love his children's mother with all his might (Ecclesiastes 9:9-10). All three of our children married young. Rob was 19 when he married, and so was Rebecca. Ricky made it to the ripe old age of 22 before he married. When I asked them why they married young, Rebecca answered, "You and Mom just made being married look like so much fun!" Of course, that's not the only reason people should consider marriage, but I'm glad that's what they remember! All the praise goes to God—and Theresa—and meeting a father named Nathan.

CHAPTER FIVE

THE INTENTIONAL FATHER

"But ye know the proof of him, that, as a son with the father, he hath served me in the gospel" (Philippians 2:22 KJV).

Having children doesn't necessarily make you a good father; "nurturing" them does. Nurturing the next generation requires intentional leadership. That's why the Apostle Paul made it a command: "And, ye fathers, provoke not your children to wrath; but bring them up in the nurture and admonition of the Lord" (Ephesians 6:4). One of my professors in Bible College used to say, "To think a thought through to the end is the hardest thing you will ever do." My Dad used to blame his lack of focus on "being too poor to pay attention." He had a point: even folks with money can suffer from that kind of poverty!

Paul's imperfections make him a wonderful example as a father. You see, there are no perfect fathers, or perfect marriages, or perfect homes. The truth is, we all need help! Most theologians believe Paul was not married and had no children. However, God chose to use him to write half the New Testament and most of the teaching on marriage and family! Since Paul didn't have a family, perhaps that explains where he found the time for his "intentional parenting" of so many in the Early Church (1 Corinthians 7:7-8, 32-33).

Abraham was the father of the faith in the Old Testament, and the Apostle Paul is referred to as a father in the New Testament. When you study Paul's relationship with his sons and daughters in the faith, none is more obvious than the young man named Timothy. Paul calls Timothy "my own son in the faith" (1 Timothy 1:2 KJV).

It appears they first met in an ancient town named Lystra. The local church elders in that region recommended Timothy to Paul. The young man must have impressed Paul, because he selected Timothy to join with his traveling missionary team (Acts 16:2-3). Timothy must have deeply trusted Paul, because he submitted to circumcision in order to travel with Paul! Ouch! (If that doesn't demonstrate Timothy's respect for Paul, then I doubt anything else would!)

Even though Timothy was already an adult, he needed and wanted a spiritual father. Paul was very intentional in their relationship. And it worked! From the very beginning, they became inseparable, and they continued to grow closer. Timothy traveled with Paul and often stayed behind in cities where Paul wanted to establish the church he had planted (Acts 17:14; Ephesians 1:3; 1 Thessalonians 3:2). Their relationship was all encompassing: Timothy stayed behind, traveled with, went before, and stood with Paul, on land and on sea (Acts 20:4). Their hearts were so knit as father and son that Paul confessed that he and Timothy were "likeminded" and "that, as a son with the father, he hath served me in the gospel" (Philippians 2:20,22 KJV).

The spiritual father and son relationship isn't something you can legislate or organize. Fathers and sons are relational, not organizational! Paul's example was more like a real dad. Paul himself said, "It's not for the children to lay up for their father, but the father to lay up for his children." A father's motive is to gladly spend and be spent for his child, even when the more abundantly he loves, the less he seems to be loved in return (2 Corinthians 12:14-19). Some ministries today abuse the role of "spiritual father" because leaders use it for personal financial gain. That's

Anyone who has raised children can testify that being a father is often a sacrificial investment of the time, training, love, and resources

a sin, a crime, and a perversion of God's design. Motive matters! Anyone who has raised children can testify that being a father is often a sacrificial investment of their time, training, love, and resources (Luke 15:11-32).

My father had several strokes that led to two major heart attacks. The last stroke crippled Dad, and he lost his ability to speak plainly. Dad died when he was only 74, but before then, my mother spent the last 16 years of Dad's life taking care of him. I stepped in and helped financially every month. I was happy to help because I loved my Dad. His last year was spent in a nursing home because he couldn't walk, swallow food, or speak plainly. Before I went to the church office every morning during the final year of Dad's life, I drove an hour round trip each day to spend time at my Daddy's bedside.

I remember the first time I shaved my father. As I put on the shaving cream, I held his sweet face in my hands just like he had held mine as a child. Daddy started crying and tears began to roll down his cheeks as I shaved him. He was unable to speak, but I knew his thoughts. I said, "Daddy, I know what you're thinking. You're embarrassed that you can't shave yourself. You remember teaching me to shave, don't you? This is just my chance to give back to you. This is no burden on me. I love you, Dad."

My Dad was a strong and proud man. It was hard to see him in a helpless condition. Many mornings, I sat in my car in the parking lot of the nursing home, weeping and praying until I could gather the emotional stability to visit him. But his strength astounded me. He always greeted me with a smile. He walked through those humbling years of weakness with great courage. In his heart, he longed to still be the provider, the protector, and the giver of purpose. The truth is, a father always desires to be the giver, even if he has nothing to give. It's our responsibility to take care of our aging parents (1 Timothy 5:8), but the heart of a true father never wants to be "burdensome" to his children. And, a faithful son will make sure his father is never made to feel that he is a burden (2 Corinthians 12:13-15).

Even when Paul was in prison awaiting execution, he continued to be a loving, attentive father to Timothy. Paul's health may have been failing. The Scriptures indicate that he was suffering from the difficult conditions of a Roman prison. Many followers had walked away from Paul because of the persecution he endured, and some left him because they were ashamed of his chains. At one point, it felt like everyone had forsaken him (2 Timothy 4:16). It appeared that Paul had outlived his usefulness for many who had once called him "father," but there was one exception: Timothy continued to love Paul. Though Paul couldn't plant churches while he was in prison, and he couldn't take Timothy on a mission trip to visit the churches they had established, Paul deserved to be respected for his chains and honored as a father—and Timothy did just that (2 Timothy 1:8)! Paul loved Timothy, and Timothy loved Paul.

Timothy honored Paul in two important ways:

First, *Timothy received Paul's instruction.*

Timothy was probably in his forties when Paul wrote him the two letters we know as First and Second Timothy. The young man had become a respected leader of leaders (1 Timothy 1:3), and Timothy received Paul's instructions and shared the letters with the churches.

Second, *Timothy kept the letters.*

This is evidence of Timothy's love for Paul, and we are blessed today that they were preserved! Their father and son relationship stands to this day as an example to us.

SUCCESSION

In Paul's first letter to Timothy, he focused on six major areas of Timothy's life. We have this example of a father's intentional leadership because Timothy honored Paul and kept his letters! These six areas are so important that I focused on them while I was raising my three children. And they continue to be my focus as I plant churches, send out pastors and missionaries, and train spiritual sons and daughters. Paul encouraged Timothy and gently led him in these six areas of life: faith, prayer, fellowship, godliness, honor, and generosity. Some people may think that raising spiritual children is different from raising naturally born sons and daughters. I would respectfully disagree. It's our privilege and responsibility as fathers to impart God's truth, God's ways, and God's purposes to our children. I call it "discipleship parenting." We can tailor the principles Paul used with Timothy to the way we raise our kids.

> These six areas are so important that I focused on them while I was raising my three children.

In the next few chapters, we'll dig into these six essential character traits that fathers can impart to their sons. By passing on these six qualities, we can ensure a successful transition—generation to generation!

CHAPTER SIX

FAITH

"The goal of this command is love, which comes from a pure heart and a good conscience and a sincere faith ... holding on to faith and a good conscience. Some have rejected these and so have shipwrecked their faith" (1 Timothy 1:5, 19 NIV).

For Theresa and me, passing on our faith began while our children were still in the womb. Theresa was always a praying woman. She and I began to fight for the faith of our children in prayer before they were born, and we've continued praying for them to this very day. Part of our prayer has always been for ourselves: that we'd be the parents our children need us to be. We wanted to teach our children about the love, forgiveness, and glory of God—and we knew that our lives needed to do the talking. Children can't hear what we're saying when our lives shout the opposite message! Theresa and I prayed for *grace to teach* our faith in Christ, *strength to live* our faith before them, and for the *Holy Spirit to impart* the faith of Jesus in them!

Like any good parent, Paul wanted his children in Christ to grow strong in faith. In our homes, we need an open Bible. This is a great responsibility on any parent, yet we can't leave the matter of passing on our faith to pastors and Sunday school teachers. Fathers must pass the baton of faith to the next generation, but we can't draw from an empty well. Our message to our children will ring hollow if our faith is not genuine.

When a father's faith is genuine, two wonderful things happen.

First, *the next generation sees our faith in our faces.*

You can be certain of this fact: children will see your faith before they'll believe it! There's nothing better than faith in action. Timothy saw the faith of his mother, Eunice, and his grandmother, Lois. The Apostle Paul confesses that he, too, had seen the faith of Timothy's mother and grandmother. Paul saw their faith before he'd seen it in Timothy. He reminded Timothy, "I am reminded of your sincere faith, which first lived in your grandmother Lois and in your mother Eunice and, I am persuaded now lives in you also" (2 Timothy 1:5 NIV).

Paul described the faith being passed through three generations—from a mother to her daughter to her grandson. But something's missing: Timothy's father and grandfather are conspicuous by their absence! Eunice and Lois must have been remarkable women.

I'm very impressed by the single mothers I've known through four decades of ministry. These women are "the grace" of the home! Solomon wrote, "A gracious woman retaineth honor" (Proverbs 11:16a KJV). She builds the home with genuine steadfast faith. It is this "unfeigned" (or genuine) trust in God that enables our faith to be passed on to the next generation. Our children are most impacted by what we do, not just what we say.

> You're circumstances at home don't have to be ideal for God to work in spiritual power.

You're circumstances at home don't have to be ideal for God to work in spiritual power. Timothy's home wasn't perfect; his dad appears to be AWOL, at least emotionally and spiritually. Whether you're a single mother or a married woman whose husband isn't a Christian, you're most effective when your walk matches your talk!

My wife's mother reminded me of Timothy's mother, Eunice. Theresa's mother had a classic Southern name: "Bobbie Jo." She gave her life to Christ when she was pregnant with Theresa, and she grew quickly in her walk with Christ. Her faithfulness to church, along with her daily love of prayer and Bible reading, produced a profound impact on her family. Her positive demeanor was even more remarkable because Bobbie Jo suffered silently for years with the pain of rheumatoid arthritis. At times, the pain and swelling were so intense that she was bedridden for seasons. When Theresa was as young as 12, she bought groceries, cleaned the house, and washed clothes for her family.

For most of their marriage, Nathan, her husband of 36 years, never went to church with Bobbie Jo. Yet her faith in Christ never wavered. Even when she knew she was dying, Bobbie Jo left this life praying in the Spirit!

The impact of her unfeigned faith speaks for itself. She passed on the faith to all four of her children. Just a couple of weeks after her passing, her husband Nathan bowed his knees in their farmhouse in Maryland and prayed. A few days later, he drove to Tennessee, where Theresa led him to the Lord. He explained, "I knew she was in Heaven, and I knew what I had to do if I wanted to see Bobbie Jo again!"

Second, *the next generation will see our faith in our focus.*

Today, people are incredibly distracted. In our homes, we need to rivet our attention on the right things: focus on the gospel, focus on grace, and shine the spotlight on Christ. You may be able to hide a lot from your friends, but your past and your personal failures are eventually going to be discovered by your children. Paul's past was never a closed book. Paul's yesterdays were constantly being brought up by his enemies. The devil accuses us to others, to ourselves, and to God (Revelation 12:10b).

The truth is, the enemy will remind us of our past to convince us to hide in a robe of hypocrisy, so don't try to run from it. Don't run, but also, don't focus on your sin—or your children's failures either. Instead, focus on the forgiveness and freedom found in the gospel! Paul admitted his past to Timothy. He confessed what he had been (1 Timothy 1:13, 15). When sin is hidden in hypocrisy, the next generation eventually finds out, and many of them walk away from the faith (vs. 7-10). Paul focused on the Gospel of God (vs. 11), and he boasted in the grace of God. Paul confessed, that God "enabled me...counted me faithful...putting me into the ministry." Paul admitted, "Christ Jesus came into the world to save sinners; of whom I am chief," and "the grace of our Lord was exceeding abundant with faith and love which is in Christ Jesus." And he confessed, "I obtained mercy" (1 Timothy 1:12-16 KJV). Paul really believed that God saved him just to prove that He could save anybody (1 Timothy 1:16)! Your faith is revealed by focusing on God's great grace, not just the law and the awfulness of sin. The law can expose sin and lead us to Christ, but it can't change a life. It simply doesn't have the power of life in it. The law can't free us from sin. We can only be free by grace through faith!

In our homes, we all have some "house rules," but we must not provoke and discourage our children by being too strict or too harsh (Colossians 3:21). Instead, fathers must fill their home with the testimony of life-changing grace, honest repentance, and second chances (Ephesians 6:4).

One of the most important statements a father can say to his family is, "I was wrong. I'm sorry. Please forgive me." I lost count of the times I had to gather my wife and children in the living room and ask for their forgiveness. I went before the church on one occasion to ask for their forgiveness. I'm not perfect, and my children know it. But they are faithfully following Jesus today because He is perfect. Keep pointing your child to Jesus. He alone can turn the heart of the next generation toward home (Luke 15:18).

Repeat the story of your salvation to the next generation. Pass on genuine "unfeigned faith." Admit it when you fail. Repent when you sin. If you're going to boast, don't boast in your works, but instead, boast of grace. And if you're looking for glory, glory in the Cross (1 Corinthians 1:29-30; Ephesians 2:9; Galatians 6:12-14)!

> One of the most important statements a father can say to his family is, "I was wrong. I'm sorry. Please forgive me."

PASSING FAITH ALONG

Last year, on October 18th, 2013, the Succession Ceremony of my pastorate took place with one of my sons: "naturally" and "in the faith." After 29 years as Senior Pastor of Calvary Church, I "passed the mantle" to a younger man. We began the 10-year transition plan in 2005. Knowing the importance of a successor ("There is no success without a successor."), we determined to prepare him in the same six areas Paul emphasized: faith, prayer, fellowship, godliness, honor, and generosity. We began our transition intentionally. I created a list with benchmarks that I called "Transition Requirements" based on my successor's development in those six areas. His developmental requirements involved faith, family, and finances. Of course, there were academic and financial benchmarks, along with incremental promotions.

My successor was like most young men. When you set before them achievable and measurable goals that lead to their destiny, they get there faster than you had expected. His future was set before him like a carrot dangling in front of a pony. He achieved all of our goals and expectations in half the 10-year window! He was ready to begin before I was ready to end!

However, faith is an immeasurable commodity in life. We had many discussions about doctrine and values, and we didn't agree on everything. No two people ever do. If I had waited until I thought he was ready in every area, we would still be waiting.

As I look back on my own life, I'm glad God used me before I was ready! I still can't comprehend why God allows me to do what I do. I was only 19 when I began preaching revivals. Why did any pastor in his right mind invite me to come? It had to be the undeserved favor of God. At age 29, I pioneered Calvary Church. Honestly, it was on the job training, yet my Heavenly Father called, equipped, and sent me. Such incredible grace! If our successor is 40 years old, and we still don't believe he's ready, then the question isn't "When?"; it's "Why haven't we already prepared them?"

WHAT DO YOU BELIEVE?

As fathers, our most important task is passing on our faith. While my successor and I were different men, we were in total agreement about what mattered. And even though we didn't agree on everything, our relationship grew deeper until I was convinced that

As fathers, our most important task is passing on our faith.

he knew my heart! I had passed on my faith. We were finally ready for succession!

Timothy was submissive to Paul's call to accountability in faith and doctrine (1 Timothy 1:4 NIV). It appears that some "desiring to be teachers of the law" had led some believers away with "unsound doctrine" in place of "the glorious gospel" (vs. 5-11). Paul urged Timothy and other sons in the faith to remain focused on salvation by grace through faith, and he used his own dramatic salvation experience as an example (vs. 12-20).

Timothy received Paul's father-like instruction about faith. Paul rejoiced that Timothy had the same heart for people that he had. Paul told the church at Philippi that he and Timothy were "likeminded" (Philippians 2:19-20 KJV). I'm sure their preaching styles were different, as well as aspects of their personalities, yet Paul had indeed passed on his faith.

Jesus explained that the Father had passed truth to Him to pass along to us: "For I have not spoken of myself; but the Father which sent me, he gave me commandment, what I should say, and what I should speak" (John 12:49 KJV). And again, "The word that you hear is not mine, but the Father's which sent me" (John 14:24 KJV). After all, Jesus is our pattern and example!

We need spiritual fathers today who are passing on the faith. Jude, the brother of Jesus, encourages us to "earnestly contend for the faith which was once delivered unto the saints" (Jude 3 KJV). This applies to our homes as well. King Solomon wrote: "Hear, ye children, the instruction of a father . . . for I give you good doctrine" (Proverbs 4:1-2 KJV).

WHAT IS FAITH?

Faith isn't simply beliefs or rules (Galatians 3:11). Faith is our way of life! Faith forms the core values that drive our decision-making. When I live by faith in the grace of God, I reveal the character of God to the next generation (Romans 1:17). Because I wasn't perfect, I needed my children to see me run to the Rock that is perfect. I needed them to see the perfect Savior living in their imperfect Dad, to see that the life I lived, I lived by the faith of the Son of God, who loved me, and gave himself for me (Galatians 2:20).

> **Because I wasn't perfect, I needed my children to see me run to the Rock that is perfect.**

Faith is more than simply a gift that we exercise to get a prayer answered. It is the revelation of the Gospel of God. Faith is core values; it is our very heart. Faith is our purpose, our passion, and our priorities. In order to pass on your faith, you invest time in those you're mentoring. We can teach ideas and ideals in a classroom, but we can only impart our vision and values through relationships. You share *what you know* through teaching, but you share *who you are* in relationships.

My Dad struggled with some bad habits from his childhood, but in spite of his failures, I knew who he wanted to be. He had passed on more than what he knew. He successfully showed me who he wanted to be! He shared his heart, not just his head—his purpose, not just his past. He gave me his absolute confidence in the finished work of the Cross. He turned my eyes from his face and pointed me to look upon Jesus!

Don't "pass the baton" until you have first "passed your faith." I knew I had transitioned to my successor my passion, purpose, and priorities. Whether you're raising children, passing on a business, or transitioning a church, the change will be much smoother if you first transition your faith. Don't just give them "the know"; also give them "the know how" and "the know why"!

The new Lead Pastor of the church I founded is my eldest son, Nathan Robert Hilton ("Robbie"). And yes, he's the one we named after my "gun-slinging" father-in-law! In some ways, it's easier when your successor is your son. In other ways, it's much more difficult. For instance, passing on faith to our children is tougher than you may think—just ask any parent of adult children! Typically, somewhere in the early teen years, children begin to question the faith, values, and priorities of their parents. It's entirely predictable, thoroughly natural, and very painful. This is why passing on our faith to our actual children is often more difficult than passing it to our "spiritual children."

As a child, I can remember thinking, "My Dad knows everything!" Then, around age 12, I thought, "Dad knows more than most." By age 16, I thought, "My friends know more than Dad." In my 20's, I thought, "I know more than Dad." At about this time, my perception of my father went into reverse. In my 30's I thought, "My Dad knows more than most." By the time I was 40, I thought, "My Dad knows everything!" Now, I just wish I could talk to him one more time!

My children, along with my sons and my daughters in the faith, have been very good to me. They have always shown me great honor and respect—so much that they made me a better son to my birth parents and my father in the faith. The way my children have valued

Theresa and me has encouraged us so much that we were convicted to make sure our parents felt that same value from us!

From one generation to the next, let's prepare our sons and daughters for their destiny and purpose. Let us pass on our faith— as our first priority!

CHAPTER SEVEN

PRAYER

"I want men everywhere to lift up holy hands in prayer,
without anger or disputing" (1 Timothy 2:8 NIV).

P rayer is life changing! Prayer is so powerful that it's not only changing lives, but also changing governments. Prayer impacts kings and kingdoms (1 Timothy 2:2). Even the spread of the Gospel message and the growth of Christ's own kingdom is a matter of prayer (Matthew 9:37-38; 1 Timothy 2:3-4). This is why a consistent example of daily prayer is one of the most important things you can pass on to the next generation. Prayer makes a believer a "change agent." According to the Scriptures, prayer has effected change in the course of planets (Joshua 10:12); the weather (1 Kings 17:1); and even length of a person's life (Isaiah 38:1-5).

Although prayer is forbidden in many places in our country and throughout the world, every person in every culture can have a rich and meaningful prayer life. Just ask Daniel (Daniel 6:6-28)! And in our "land of the free," you don't have to limit prayer to Sunday mornings at church. You can still pray at home, in your car, or simply under your breath. Prayer is one privilege no man can refuse you. You can pray for the president or the governor, the clerk at the grocery store, or the pizza delivery boy. And the beauty of prayer is that it is available to "men everywhere" (verse 8)!

THE POWER OF AN EXAMPLE

My wife is a wonderful woman of prayer. Her mother passed on the blessing of prayer to her. When Theresa and her siblings were small, her mother would take them into her bedroom to pray. Bobbie Jo would set them on her bed, close the door, and pray sometimes for hours. Theresa still remembers her mother's prayers for her father's salvation. Her father didn't come to know Christ until after her mother passed away, but even death couldn't hinder the fulfillment of her fervent prayer. After she died, her prayer for Nathan continued to live upon the altar of God (Revelation 8:2-3)! No wonder Theresa is leaving such a powerful example of prayer for our children. She saw it in her mother.

Some of our best prayer times with our children took place on the way home from church. One Wednesday night, the presence of God was so strong in our car as we prayed that Theresa unbuckled her seatbelt, turned around, and laid her hand on the foreheads of our three children. She then began to pray prophetically concerning their future and their destinies. When we arrived at home, we stayed in the car for another half hour praying. The windows fogged up as Theresa and I, together with our children, wept and continued praying. God has fulfilled every one of those prayers (Genesis 49:1). These moments in the presence of God marked our children for God.

The next generation must hear our voices lifted up in sincere, fervent prayer. When God answers those prayers, they will witness firsthand the power of prayer, and most importantly, the reality and accessibility of our God! They must know that He is as near as their next breath (Romans 10:8-10).

Jesus left us a pattern life of prayer and lessons on how to pray (Luke 11:1). Even though He is God's Son, Jesus felt the need to pray! The sound of His voice in prayer and the immediate presence of the Heavenly Father caused the disciples to want to pray like Jesus prayed.

I know how the disciples felt. I can still hear my own father and mother praying. My Dad's voice was always fervent and confident in prayer. Dad would stand and pray. Sometimes he would pace back and forth. It seemed as if he knew the Lord was right there walking with him, listening and responding! My mother, Anna Lee, was more imploring as she prayed. She often wept in strong intercession for others. Her prayer posture was different than Dad's. While he was standing, my mother was kneeling or on her face. She often prayed for hours.

We moved a lot when I was a child, but you could count on Mom to do two things in each house we lived: she made each house feel like a home, and she found a private place of prayer. Once, she made a place of prayer in the basement, and I overheard her calling out my name. When I was 16, I had been running from the Lord. I was in rebellion and wouldn't surrender my life to Christ. As I stood by the door at the top of the basement stairs, I heard her praying, "Oh mighty God, whatever You must do to save Richard's soul from Hell, do it! Place someone beside him that will boldly testify to him. Take away his appetite, disturb his sleep with dreams of Hell and Your Second Coming until he repents and is saved from sin!"

I remember thinking, "Oh my God! Please Mom, take it easy!" I was alarmed because I knew in my heart that God would surely answer her prayers. By the time I was 17, I had been apprehended by grace and yielded my life to Christ through the prayers of my mother!

It's the responsibility of all parents and spiritual fathers to pray for their children—and to teach them how to pray. Jesus taught the disciples "that men ought always to pray" (Luke 18:1 KJV), and again, "Watch ye therefore, and pray always" (Luke 21:36 KJV). Even though He was the Son of God, Jesus left the example of a consistent, daily prayer life. Jesus prayed in the early mornings (Mark 1:35), in the evenings (Mark 6:46), and all night long (Luke 6:12). Jesus prayed privately (Mark 1:35; Luke 5:16), in small groups (Luke 9:18), and in public (Matthew 11:25; John 17).

Jesus prayed so fervently in The Garden of Gethsemane that the small capillaries near the surface of His skin burst under the stress until His sweat looked like great drops of blood! Jesus became so weak from this prayer that an angel came and ministered strength to him (Luke 22:43-44).

I'm convinced that the lack of intercessory prayer for the next generation causes delayed spiritual maturity in our children and in our sons in the faith. Recent studies reveal that pastors in the United States average only minutes in prayer each week. And that's the pastors! It's frightening to imagine how little prayer is going on in Christian homes!

The Apostle Paul prayed intensely for the growth of his children in the faith. In his letter to the Galatians, he wrote, "My little children, of whom I travail in birth again until Christ be formed in you" (Galatians 4:19 KJV). Jesus told Peter, "Satan hath desired to have you, that he may sift you as wheat; but I have prayed for thee, that thy faith fail not" (Luke 22:31-32 KJV).

I'm convinced that the lack of intercessory prayer for the next generation causes delayed spiritual maturity in our children and in our sons in the faith.

To neglect prayer is the height of spiritual pride. It's confidence in the flesh. How can we encourage the next generation to pray if we fail to pray? When we pray, we reveal our humility and our humanity to our children. If we have prayed, then we rightly give God the glory and praise for every answered prayer and success in life. When we pray, we point our children toward the Source of our faith, our family, and our future!

As we raise our children, let's teach them why we pray. During the years my children lived at home, they were witnesses to my consistent need for daily prayer and devotional time. My daughter Rebecca recently told a friend, "My brothers and I knew where Dad would be every morning. We would find him at the dining table praying and reading his Bible." When my children asked me why I prayed so much, I answered, "I *must* pray. Your Daddy needs the strength he finds in prayer!" Each day I would pray individual prayers over them for that day. On the way to school, I'd find out the events of that day and pray out loud, calling out their names to God before they got out of the car. Monday nights were set aside as family prayer night. I considered our private prayer time in our home a greater priority than the corporate prayer gatherings at the church.

Whatever it takes, whatever has to be rearranged in your schedule, teach your children to pray! You will teach them to pray by letting them watch and listen as you pray, and as you invite them to join you.

PRAYING WITH OUR FAMILY

There are two obvious benefits we gain from praying with our spouse and children.

First, *hearing others pray encourages and challenges us.*

My mother is 76 years old, and it blesses me to hear her voice in prayer. Theresa's voice is always filled with such faith when she prays. But I can't describe the emotions that flood my heart when

I hear my children pray! One of the things I miss most since I left the pastorate is hearing the voices of the elders and pastoral team lifted high in fervent prayer. We live in a day when many congregations have never heard their pastor pray, and many children have never heard their parents lift up their voices in prayer. If we want to build a life of faith and prayer in our children, they have to hear us pray.

A second benefit of our children hearing our family pray is: *Others hearing us pray helps us avoid "vain repetition"* (Matthew 6:7 KJV).

Vain repetition is when we habitually use the same old phrases over and over—and over again. One night I was praying for my daughter Rebecca when she was only 7 years old. As I tucked her in for bedtime prayers, she was listening intently to me pray. She suddenly interrupted me and said, "Daddy, you're praying your supper prayer. You just asked God to bless this food set before us!" Needless to say, I paid closer attention to the remainder of that prayer, and I tried to come up with a sincere, original "supper prayer" the next day at dinner!

PRAYING WITH OUR CHURCH

During my 29 years as pastor, we began each year in January with 21 days of prayer and fasting. I believed that if we sought God and gave Him the first fruits of the year, He would bless the remainder of the year with passion, power, and purpose. And He did! Every year the church grew numerically, financially, and spiritually. It wasn't a legalistic thing. It was a simple matter of pursuit. Prayer isn't about the pursuit of possessions; it's the pursuit of a Person. You don't have to pursue His hands when you're seeking His face! It's the Father's "good pleasure to give you the kingdom" (Luke 12:32 KJV). It's about relationship, not works. We are His "offspring" and we just want to seek Him (Acts 17:27-28).

There are many wonderful blessings available to the praying church. Let's glance together at just two.

First, *agreeing together for God's promises.*

The New Testament Christian church began with 24/7 prayer. These early church believers gathered "in one mind" and "in one accord" to pray for "the promise of the Father," the power of the Holy Spirit (Acts 1:14).

Prayer isn't about the pursuit of possessions; it's the pursuit of a Person.

Second, *boldness to continue the vision.*

The enemy of our souls opposes the efforts of any local church, because he knows we are more successful when we focus on our vision in unity. The early church believers often gathered to ask God to grant them boldness to continue doing what He had called them to do (Acts 4:24).

PRAYING FOR THE NEXT GENERATION

Paul held his son Timothy accountable for his prayer life as a man of God (1 Timothy 2:1-8). We too, must hold before the next generation a steadfast example of prayer. There are several reasons that praying for our children is both beneficial and necessary. I will mention only two.

First, pray for them because *the next generation needs God's direction on their lives!* (2 Corinthians 4:1, 5-7)

God alone gives us an eternal and compelling purpose. God has a plan, a future, and a hope for each of our children. We need prayer because, like Moses, we have to communicate with the One in "the burning bush"! How can anyone know "what I should say, and what I should speak" without hearing the Heavenly Father's instruction (John 12:49)? In humility we acknowledge the grace and mercy of God upon our future. "God blesses those who realize their need for him, for the kingdom of Heaven is given to them" (Matthew 5:3 NLT). I continue to pray for direction in my life and theirs. If you're not praying, you're not listening! And if you're not listening, you won't hear God's voice speaking "a word behind thee, saying, 'This is the way, walk ye in it, when ye turn to the right hand, and when ye turn to the left'" (Isaiah 30:21 KJV). God promises to make your path clear, to direct every step, and to delight in every detail of life—for you and for your children (Psalm 37:23-26).

Second, pray for them because *the next generation will need God's super on their natural!*

Paul admitted that his public speaking ability wasn't "all that and a bag of chips." He confessed his need for God to anoint his words (1 Corinthians 2:4). No matter what talents, experiences, or skill set our children have, God can anoint them with His Spirit. When God places His super on our natural it becomes *supernatural!* When Moses needed a carpenter to build the Tabernacle and its furniture, the Lord instructed him to use a man named Bezaleel because God had filled "him with the Spirit of God, giving him great wisdom, intelligence, and skill in all kinds of crafts" (Exodus 31:3 NLT). Fathers, we must teach the next generation to humbly pray, admitting their need for His power on their natural talents and abilities. God can give them a heavenly advantage in an earthly situation. King David wrote these words of confidence and a plea: "The Lord will work out His plans for my life.... Don't abandon me, for you made me" (Psalm 138:8 NLT).

When mothers and fathers pray, God will guide them concerning their children's natural gifts and abilities. We can help them identify their calling—what they are capable of and what they do well. The Bible instructs parents: "Train up a child in the way he should go" (Proverbs 22:6 NLT), or "Teach your children to choose the right path." Our children are like arrows. We can point them toward the bull's eye in their natural gifts and release them in the right direction. We are blessed when our "quiver is full of them" (Psalm 127:4-5 NLT).

> When mothers and fathers pray, God will guide them concerning their children's natural gifts and abilities.

God revealed to Theresa and me the skills and destiny of each of our children. Our youngest, Rebecca, was gifted in administration. By her junior year of high school, she was working in the Guidance Counselors office. She was a problem solver. (This was trouble when she tried to fix her brothers!) Today, she's in accounting and is Operations Manager of the Washington County Economic Development Council.

Our youngest son, Ricky was a born musician, actor, and singer. He's been rocking since he was a baby in his car seat! Because of his gift, he was able to pay his own way through college. Today, he is a Worship Pastor. Rick composes beautiful, Christ-centered worship music.

Our oldest son, Robbie, tripped me up. He was always an exceptional athlete, and I assumed he would go into professional sports. His team named him "the heart and soul" of their team. I saw an athlete, but God saw a pastor.

That is exactly why we must pray. Sometimes we see a shepherd boy when God sees a king (1 Samuel 16:7). If we pray, God will direct their steps . . . and our leadership. Most of the time, their destiny may be obvious. At other times, the future is most uncertain. This is why every parent, and certainly every spiritual father, should take the responsibility of the next generation's destiny to God in prayer! Ask God to place His Spirit upon their destiny and their gifts—and be sure to pass on a passion for prayer.

CHAPTER EIGHT

FELLOWSHIP

"Although I hope to come to you soon, I am writing you these instructions
so that, if I am delayed, you will know how people ought to conduct
themselves in God's household, which is the church of the living God,
the pillar and foundation of the truth" (1 Timothy 3:15 NIV).

Paul demonstrates how to intentionally pour life into our sons and daughters. He began by passing on his faith to Timothy. Then, he passed on his passion for prayer. Now, Paul focuses on the importance of worship and fellowship in the church. As I prepared my successor to transition into the pastoral role, I rejoiced to see his faith grow and his prayer life intensify. Observing how he loved God's house and God's people gave me great confidence moving forward. But the principles of worship and fellowship aren't restricted to pastors. All of us are called to "worship the Lord in the spirit of holiness."

One of the best blessings we can give our children is a love for the House of God. I realize the church is people. Some are quick to point out that we should love people and not the church, but even casual reading of the Scriptures will reveal that we can love both the place we worship *and* the people who call it home!

As a matter of fact, Jesus demonstrated love for both the people and the place as He entered Jerusalem at the beginning of the last week of His earthly life. Palm Sunday's Triumphal Entry was followed by a revelation of His love for His house and for people. First, Jesus called the Temple "My house" and chased the corrupt leaders out of the building. He loved the place! Jesus' zeal was coupled with deep compassion. After cleansing the Temple, Jesus healed the lame and the blind. The children entered God's house as well, singing and worshiping the Lord (Matthew 21:12-16). The children received a great blessing by being in the Lord's house. They worshiped and spent time in the presence of Jesus.

Although Jesus had little time left, He went to the Temple every day of Passion Week (Luke 19:47). Shouldn't we have His same love for His people and for His house?

The religious leaders were angry that Jesus welcomed and ministered to the sick. They also were angry with the children because of the loud and joyful praise! What a shame! We should want the next generation to experience the manifold blessings of Jesus. Let's teach them to love the local church.

TEACH THEM TO GET INVOLVED

As a father in the faith, the Apostle Paul encouraged people to "desire" involvement in the local church. He referred to the desire to be a leader in the church as "a good work." When we get involved in church, it's a great example to our children (1 Timothy 3:1a KJV). The phrase "a good work" is also translated "a noble task" (NIV), "an excellent task" (AMP), and "a fine work" (NAS). One of the best things parents can do is to be faithful to and involved in their local church!

Jesus tells the story of a young man who grew up in his father's house. When he became a man, he demanded his inheritance, left home, and got involved in terrible sins. One day he remembered how wonderful it was back at his father's house, and he returned home willing to serve there (Luke 15:17-20). What a wonderful promise! Our children will return to God if we fill their hearts with good memories of the Lord's house. We should love the house of God, speak well of the house of God, and be faithful to the house of God … for our children's sake!

SPEAK HIGHLY OF CHURCH LEADERS

Paul described the offices of elder and deacon with high words of praise. He described the men who fill those positions as men of the highest character. He said they were to be blameless, faithful in marriage, and with great self-control. He added that these leaders are respectable and led their families well. Wow! The bar is raised pretty high for these spiritual leaders, but we need to remember that leaders are people, too! That's why we should give them room for some humanity.

We must be careful to speak well of church leaders before our children. When we trash our church and fill our homes with negative talk about the leaders in our churches, it should come as no surprise when our children want nothing to do with God's house. Even when they're young, they're listening! Today, the number of youth raised in church that leave when they become adults is staggering! The Barna Group reports that 6 out of 10 young people leave the church and never return. There may be many different reasons, but one of them is that they hear their parents disparage the

> When we trash our church and fill our homes with negative talk about the leaders in our churches, it should come as no surprise when our children want nothing to do with God's house.

church and its leaders. When we get involved in church activities, worship with all our hearts, enjoy it, and speak highly of the church and the people, we create a positive environment for our kids, and many will want to stay connected to the house of God. Children want to be part of the things that bring joy to their parents and security to their parents' marriage. Take an inventory of the messages you give your children about church and the leaders, and make any changes that are necessary to create an affirming, thankful, faith-filled atmosphere.

Theresa's mother loved her local church, and she always spoke highly of it, the people, and the pastor. Bobbie Jo was actively involved as the pianist. She also made the best potato salad this side of Heaven for the church dinners! She did all that and still made Nathan, her unsaved husband, feel like a man! Theresa's parents were married 36 years, and her Dad never went to church with her Mom. But because of Bobbie Jo's high praise of God's house, he loved her church!

Once, the local mechanic put Nathan's respect for his wife's church to a test. Nathan had taken his truck to be repaired, but the mechanic seemed to have a problem with the church Bobbie Jo attended. When he voiced his criticism, Nathan told him, "You need to stop talking about my wife's church and fix my truck!" His warning was ignored, and the mechanic kept criticizing the church. Once more, Nathan spoke up: "Harley, this is your last chance. Stop talking about my wife's church and fix my truck!" (Actually, Harley wasn't the man's name. Nathan called anyone who got on his nerves, "Harley." I have no idea why.) Once more, the mechanic ignored the warning. By this time, the mechanic was laying on a flat dolly under the truck. As the man's next round of criticism began, Nathan suddenly grabbed the mechanics feet, pulled him out from under the truck, punched him in the mouth, shoved him back under the truck and yelled, "I told you to stop running down my wife's church and fix my truck!"

I don't recommend punching out the people who say ugly things about your church. The point is: an unsaved spouse loved his wife's church! She hadn't spoken a negative word about her church, so that even after her death, there was no lingering animosity toward the Lord in her husband's heart! Nathan eventually became a Christian, and all four of Bobbie Jo's children love God, His people, and His house!

You don't have to argue, gripe, complain, and push people into going to church with you. Just love God, love people, and love your church. Love is contagious. Eventually, like the story Jesus told, even those who drift away from God will someday return to the Father's house! Your unsaved friend, spouse, relative, and co-worker will eventually come to visit the church you speak highly of!

> **Just love God, love people, and love your church. Love is contagious.**

SPEAK WELL OF YOUR CHURCH IN YOUR COMMUNITY

Paul described the kind of reputation good leaders have throughout the community: "Also, people outside the church must speak well of him" (1 Timothy 3:7a NLT). We all want our community to think highly of our church, and it all begins with you and me. Instead of finding fault with anything and everything—and delighting in telling others about it—we need to talk highly of each other. We can actually help our community's perception of our church and its leaders by speaking words of honor and affirmation. Satan is "the accuser of the brethren" (Revelation 12:10b KJV), and the devil doesn't need any help from us. Don't join in with him!

I love to see people's eyes light up as they talk about their church, their pastor, and the people in their churches. Quite often, a spirit of gratitude starts at the top. I always select leaders who consistently speak well of the church and one another. These instructions aren't just requirements for church leaders; they are describing the testimony every Christian should possess! All believers should want their lives and homes to speak for Jesus— to reveal Jesus to their community. In other words, we represent the King to everyone who's watching!

As a father, my values were always on display. I wanted my children to understand that my motive for Christ-like living wasn't so that I could keep my job or get a leadership position at church. Instead, I wanted my life to please God and to point my children and my city to Christ!

But I knew that I couldn't live a flawless life. I knew that my staff couldn't do that either. As I mentored my successor and the next generation, I gave room to our leaders for failure. I walked side-by-side with leaders to the other side of their failures. I forgave, I went the extra mile, and I've never regretted it! The Old Law dealt harshly with failure. It was "an eye for an eye" (Matthew 5:38 KJV), and called for revenge, restitution, and retribution. Jesus taught a New Law of Love (Matthew 5:39-48; John 13:34), which called for repentance, restoration, and reconciliation. There's a big difference! The hope of forgiveness and second chances

The hope of forgiveness and second chances draws flawed people to the church and gives us our "voice" in the city.

draws flawed people to the church and gives us our "voice" in the city. You see, love has a voice. Love has a name. Love has a testimony! Jesus said: "By this shall all men know that ye are my disciples, if ye have love one to another" (John 13:35 KJV). Love speaks ... loudly!

I looked for leaders with this special touch of grace. This kind of merciful love and grace in our leadership didn't hurt our church's influence in our city—it expanded it. No leader is flawless, and no church is perfect. All of us need God's forgiveness and restoration— we just need to be honest about our need! It's grace that stands as a beacon of hope to our communities, not criticism and legalism. In our church, we knew that if we would just love God, love each other, and love His house, we could at least point the lost to the Source of our love! When we fell, we got back up and kept moving forward. When we blew it, we repented and accepted God's grace and kept moving forward. True repentance is incredibly powerful and attractive.

SELECTING GOOD LEADERS

When my children lived at home, I was very involved in their choice of friends. Every parent knows the impact and influence of friendships upon their children. Solomon wrote, "He that walketh with wise men shall be wise: but a companion of fools shall be destroyed" (Proverbs 13:20 KJV). That's why selecting the right friends is perhaps the most critical training any father will give a son in the faith. This principle is true for young children, older children, adults, and church leadership—relationships matter! We are prone to suddenly place someone in a position because of an existing, pressing need, but Paul admonished Timothy to "lay hands suddenly on no man" (1 Timothy 5:22a KJV). Paul gave his son in the faith clear counsel in the selection of leaders. Paul didn't overstep his authority by selecting the leaders for Timothy, but he gave the young man clear instructions and guidelines. He described the kind of men that would make good leaders. By the way, for every parent reading this, these are also the kind of people that make good friends for you, too—and your child!

THE REASONS WE NEED GOOD LEADERSHIP

Before we describe a good friend or a good leader, let's first look at why we need them. Moses is a great example. He needed leaders for three reasons:

First, *he could do a better job with some help.*

He admitted, "I am not able to bear all this people alone, because it is too heavy for me" (Numbers 11:14 KJV). Because Moses had help, the people received more personal and hands-on care.

Second, *he could live longer with some help.*

Moses was under such weight that he asked God, just "kill me" (Numbers 11:15a KJV). I would have loved to see the results of Moses' stress test! It's true: we all need a friend, a helper, a sheltering tree.

Third, *he could share the burden with those who helped him.*

We all need someone to "stand there" with us and share our same "spirit," our same heart and our same passions. Joys are doubled and burdens are halved with someone by our side (Numbers 11:16-17 KJV).

LIKEMINDED

When you're certain that a potential leader (or a maturing son or daughter) has your heart, you can begin to look for the traits of leadership that Paul describes. It's important that the pastor and the leaders work together in unity. A team will become unproductive when the leaders are qualified—when they "seek their own" agendas. Without unity of vision and purpose, the care for the people becomes inconsistent and insincere. That's why the leadership team must have "the same spirit" as their pastor, and children soak up the values of their parents. Paul called it being "likeminded."

This is very important for a successful transition—in leadership in the church, and to adulthood for all children. If you transition your heart into your Successor, then you can build a team that has his heart. Paul was able to send Timothy in his stead to the church at Philippi, because Timothy would "naturally care" for them just like Paul (Philippians 2:19-21 NKJV). This harmony makes the "burden of the people" much easier to bear and the care of the people "natural" and genuine!

TRAITS OF A GOOD LEADER

In Exodus 18:21 and Acts 6:3, Moses and Luke agree in a summary of the traits of good leaders. They must be:

» *Men of truth.* They need to be honest men, so select those with integrity. Again, they won't be flawless, but they must be honest with you and with themselves.

» *Men of ability.* They should be Spirit-filled. To be filled with God's Spirit and power, they have to realize they're empty on their own. The Holy Spirit puts the "super" on their natural!

» *Men who fear God.* They need to be wise. Men who don't fear God won't respect you!

» *Men without a personal agenda.* In other words, they "hate covetousness." They don't covet what others on the team have and they aren't jealous of another's popularity or skills. They need to be good team players.

In addition, Paul added a very important factor to the list of Moses and Luke in the selection of leaders. He included the spouse and the condition of the marriage and family (1 Timothy 3:4-5,11-12). Whether it is a friendship, family member, business partner, or church leader, your relationship will be impacted by the person's spouse—count on it! Choose and mentor a successor with a strong family. Be certain the marriage is prepared for the transition.

Teach the next generation, our sons and daughters, to love God's people and God's house. Teach the next generation to speak highly of the church and the people who call your local church home. Theresa's mother did, and it changed the destiny of her spouse and her children! Years after her father's salvation, Theresa asked Nathan if he had any regrets in 36 years of marriage to Bobbie Jo. Nathan answered: "Only one. I deeply regret that I never went to church with your mother!"

CHAPTER NINE

GODLINESS

"For physical training is of some value, but godliness has value for all things, holding promise for both the present life and the life to come" (1 Timothy 4:7 NIV).

Paul was concerned about the physical health of his young son in the faith, but even more, he wanted him to become spiritually strong. Apparently, Timothy had some nagging health problems, including frequent stomach and digestion issues, and that he was "often" sick (1 Timothy 5:23 KJV). All parents want their children to live a long healthy life. That's why Paul encouraged Timothy to live life with personal discipline, to exercise both physically and spiritually.

My Dad's health rapidly declined in his late 50's. He suffered multiple strokes and several heart attacks the last 20 years of his life. A contributing factor was the alcoholism of his youth. Also, he suffered from Post Traumatic Stress Syndrome, PTSD. Dad was only 16 when he arrived in Japan just weeks after the atomic bombs had fallen. Later, he was wounded in fierce combat in Korea, where he saw his best friend die. In addition, his health problems were compounded by a long-term smoking habit that damaged his lungs and heart. After he got sick, I desperately wanted to see him healthy.

PERSONAL DISCIPLINE

Now that I'm a grandfather, I pray for the health of my children and grandchildren. I can identify with Paul's loving concern for his son in the faith. One of the keys to long life is discipline. We must discipline our bodies and our spirits. To optimize our chances at a long and healthy life, we must take care of ourselves spiritually, physically, and emotionally. We are body, soul, and spirit (1 Thessalonians 5:23 KJV), and we must live a balanced life. We want that for our children—and for our parents and ourselves!

On March 21st, 2004, my granddaughter Aaliyah was born. Two days later, I wrote in my prayer journal some thoughts that reflect my desire for the health of those I love:

> "Good morning, Lord. Aaliyah went home from the hospital with Robbie and Monica this morning, and I was there! What an odd mix of emotions this morning. First, I visited Dad at the nursing home, and then I ran to see his newborn great-granddaughter. They have a few things in common: they both were bathed and dressed by another, both in diapers, both dressed in their sleeping garments, both unable to eat solid food, etc. One just arrived in this world, the other is nearing the opposite shore, but both are here with purpose!"

One of the key motivators for living a spiritually and physically disciplined life is understanding the impact our lives have on others. Paul told Timothy two very good reasons to watch his life closely: others are watching, and it could save their lives (1 Timothy 4:16)!

EXERCISING GODLINESS

Evidently, Timothy was already involved in some aspects of physical discipline—perhaps because of his health issues. Paul acknowledged the benefits of physical exercise and encouraged him to apply that same discipline to his spiritual life by exercising godliness. Godliness isn't obscure or hard to understand—it's obedience to God's Word! Paul took it a step further and instructed Timothy that exercising godliness was a greater priority than physical exercise and held even greater benefits (1 Timothy 4:7-8).

As parents, it's our responsibility to establish the priority of godly living in the hearts of our children. Unfortunately, many parents in our culture travel for hours and spend a small fortune taking their children to practices and sporting events, but they complain about the time spent in church! We may talk as if the church is the most important thing, but our watch, our words, and our wallet reveal a different priority—and our children know it. We need to exercise godly discipline in order to successfully transition our faith, prayer life, and love for Christ into the lives of our children.

One of the key motivators for living a spiritually and physically disciplined life is understanding the impact our lives have on others.

In the same way that certain exercises help us in specific ways (like sit-ups strengthening our abdominal muscles), Paul describes certain spiritual disciplines that develop godliness. Of course, "exercising godliness" as Paul called it (verse 7) isn't something we do to be saved. The Christian is already right with God by faith in Jesus and His finished work on the Cross. However, the benefits of spiritual disciplines are spiritual strength and growth. I focused on training my children in spiritual discipline by my example. The aspects of this discipline include several components:

First, *hunger for God's Word* (1 Timothy 4:11).

We need to read the Word of God, hear it, and teach its principles to our children. There are so many voices speaking into their ears. Teachers, coaches, friends, online sites, and other literature shape their worldview. We're influenced by what we read as much as by what we hear and see. Fill your home with great Christian literature.

Someone once said we have two dogs living inside us: one is a mean, selfish, "junkyard dog," and the other is a pleasant and playful golden retriever. The two dogs are constantly fighting one another for control. The one we feed the most will become the strongest. Paul described this conflict by saying, "For the good that I would I do not: but the evil which I would not, that I do" (Romans 7:19 KJV). The answer is to feed your spirit with the good Word of God (Ephesians 6:10-17).

One of my fondest memories growing up was visiting my grandparents, William and Nellie Byrd. My grandfather, "Papaw Bill," left me with three distinct memories. One was his sweet nature. He was so sweet that his sweetness had a witness—Juicy Fruit chewing gum! Whenever we visited, Papaw would always give us a stick of gum. Second, he sang in the church choir and he had a very distinctive nasal tenor voice that stood out—it really stood out! I always admired the grace of the choir. My third important memory is his open Bible. Grandma would open the door and as our family came from the front porch through the screen door into the living room, and there was Papaw Bill, sitting in his chair with his Bible open on his lap. I'll never forget my grandfather's Bible. Now, five generations later, his grandchildren's grandchildren still read its timeless truths. Times change, people vacillate, cultures shift, but God's Word never changes!

Secondly, *obey God's Word* (1 Timothy 4:12-15).

We need to model God's truths in our daily lives. Paul instructed Timothy to "command and teach" the Scriptures, but that's not enough. He must also be "an example to all believers in what you teach, in the way you live."

For good or ill, we're examples to those who are watching us. Wayward fathers often reproduce wayward children. Had the prodigal's father been unfaithful, who would the son have come home to? We must be fathers in the faith who practice what we preach! That is exactly why we must exercise the spiritual man. As they say down at the gym, "Eat right and exercise." Spiritually, we devour God's Word and exercise obedience to Him.

Paul tells Timothy to "give attendance to reading," but more importantly, to exercise biblical principles and give yourself "wholly to them" so that everyone will see your personal spiritual progress (1 Timothy 4:15 KJV). Our children need to see us reading the Bible and practicing (exercising) its principles in our daily lives. One way or another, they will follow our example.

Third, *desire spiritual gifts*.

Paul instructed Timothy to use the gift that God had given him. God has given every believer gifts, talents, and abilities (Romans 12:6; 1 Corinthians 12:7,31). By "reason of use," our gifts mature and become more effective (Hebrews 5:14 KJV).

The origin of every good and perfect gift in our lives is God (James 1:17). Gifts can be *inherited*, *inspired*, and *imparted*. First, some gifts are inherited. God gave some talents to us when we were born. It's a fact that our very DNA has latent propensities. This explains why we're born with certain strengths (as well as particular weaknesses). For instance, I've inherited my Dad's poor eyesight, but I also inherited his rugged good looks! Secondly, some gifts are inspired. Watching others love and serve God gives us a passion to follow their example. Teachers, mentors, and coaches inspire. Spiritual parents and a loving, faith-filled home provide the best environment for inspiration.

In the same way that some gifts are inherited and inspired, some gifts are imparted. God suddenly and supernaturally can give us an ability through prayer. Paul spoke of that kind of gift when he told Timothy: "Neglect not the gift that is in thee, which was given thee by prophecy, with the laying on of the hands of the presbytery" (1 Timothy 4:14 KJV). And again, "Wherefore I put thee in remembrance that thou stir up the gift of God, which is in thee by the putting on of my hands" (2 Timothy 1:6 KJV).

Theresa experienced the impartation of a spiritual gift when she was 12 years old. Her mother had been the church pianist for years, but she had also been fighting a battle with rheumatoid arthritis. The condition grew so severe in her hands that she could no longer play because of the pain. They sat down at the piano, and Bobbie Jo placed her hands on Theresa's hands. She prayed that God would impart the gift to play piano to her—and Theresa immediately began to play! Theresa has always wondered why God answered that prayer, while her prayers for her mothers healing weren't answered. We may never know in this life. However, we know that every generation has the responsibility of developing the gifts God gives their children (Proverbs 22:6). Whether our gift was imparted, inspired, or inherited, we need to help our children develop them for Christ's purpose.

AVOID NEGLECTING GIFTS, TALENTS, AND ABILITIES

Paul told Timothy, "Neglect not the gift" (1 Timothy 4:14a KJV). Neglect is always destructive. It's the waste of potential and always results in loss. For instance, neglect exercise and lose your health, neglect the farm and lose a harvest, neglect a business and lose the profit, neglect a spouse and lose a marriage, neglect a garden and lose the fruit, neglect a child and lose a legacy!

No wonder Paul invested so much of himself into his children in the faith! Because he invested in the spiritual sons he was raising up, they in turn preserved his parchments, propagated his passion, and pursued his purpose (2 Timothy 2:2; 4:2,13). When a father helps develop the gifts in his children, he's investing in his own legacy. The successful development of the next generation is the greatest kind of success!

> Paul invested so much of himself into his children in the faith! Because he invested in the spiritual sons he was raising up, they in turn preserved his parchments, propagated his passion, and pursued his purpose.

The most formidable opponent of neglect is godly personal discipline. We receive so much from a parent, but the development of the gift is each person's responsibility! In essence, let me paraphrase Paul's words to Timothy: "God gave you genuine faith through your grandmother and mother, God gave you a gift through me, now don't neglect it" (2 Timothy 1:5-6; 3:15)!

Exercising godliness isn't a "law thing." It's not works in exchange for salvation. Instead, the motive is obedience out of the heartfelt experience of God's amazing grace. This produces service from a saved and grateful heart. Instead of fear, pride, or shame, the motivation to obey is to demonstrate love and loyalty to the One who has rescued us! Personal discipline is exercising faith in Christ's decision to use you. It's faith in Christ in you (Galatians 2:20).

In Matthew's Gospel, Jesus described our personal responsibility as a step of faith. He told the parable of a great and wealthy man who went away to a far country. Before leaving, he entrusted all of his wealth to the care of his servants. Some servants had more gifts and talents than others, but everyone had been given something of value from their master. When the master returned, he called all his servants to give an account of what they had done with their gifts. Interestingly, the ones with the most to lose had taken the risk to invest what he had entrusted to them. Their investments became profitable, and they increased their master's kingdom. Of course, this parable is about our Master and the many resources He has put into our hands. Jesus desires that we use the gifts He's given us to expand His kingdom. Simply put, the purpose of developing and exercising your gift is evangelism!

However, one poor fellow in the parable decided not to use his gift. In fear, and trusting only himself, he failed to take the risk. He dug a hole and hid his talent. Neglected and hidden away, his gift didn't multiply. Profitless, his talent lay wasting, hidden, useless and neglected. Christ's kingdom was not expanding (Matthew 25:25-30).

As I trained my sons in the faith, I took my responsibility seriously. I knew that training involves instruction and example. I couldn't just say, "Do as I say." I understood that my walk had to match my talk. Jesus told His disciples: "Follow me" (Mark 2:14 KJV). Paul asked his children in the faith to "be followers together of me" and also, "Those things, which ye have both learned, and received, and heard, and seen in me, do" (Philippians 3:17; 4:9 KJV).

As you pass down your faith, prayer life, and love for God's house, be sure you're personally using your gifts and living a godly disciplined life. After all, before your children can "do," they must first "learn, receive, hear, and see it in you"!

CHAPTER TEN

HONOR

"Do not sharply rebuke an older man; but rather appeal to him as a father, to the younger men as brothers, the older women as mothers, and the younger women as sisters, in all purity. Honor widows who are widows indeed" (1 Timothy 5:1-3 NAS).

Honor is a seed. When we sow honor and respect into the soil of another person's life, a bountiful harvest of honor will eventually come back to us. The younger we are when we begin to sow honor, the earlier we begin to see the harvest of honor. Honor begins at home. Paul reminded the church at Ephesus, "Honor your father and mother—which is the first commandment with a promise—that it may go well with you and that you may enjoy long life on the earth. Fathers, do not exasperate your children, instead, bring them up in the training and instruction of the Lord" (Ephesians 6:2-3 NIV).

Honor is an essential tool in training a successor and preparing the next generation for their destiny. Paul took the time to teach Timothy the meaning of honor and how to show it in his relationships. The churches Paul and Timothy had founded were very young and filled with baby Christians! And the churches were cross-cultural. Christianity was for every man and woman—no exceptions. Various races, multiple ethnic groups and nationalities had begun to worship together for the first time in history. The blood of Jesus had broken down the walls separating men and women, Jews and Gentiles, slaves and free men. Christianity was changing the world, and history was being made in the church. Change came with a price tag. During this radical social transition, Paul encountered strife, division, and envy from Corinth to Galatia to Ephesus (1Corinthians 1:10-12; Galatians 2:11-14; 3:26-29; Ephesians 2:14-17, 4:29-32; etc.).

The infant Christian churches were filled with diversity. Paul was a true father in the faith. He went about sowing seeds of honor and respect, but the lack of honor in those churches wasn't simply along ethnic and cultural divides. No matter the culture, it appears the younger men didn't know how to properly respect the older men and women in the church. As a matter of fact, the young Christian men of Ephesus needed more than a little help, it seems they didn't know how to treat each other—or the young Christian women!

To further complicate the matter, the older men had responded to the disrespect by dishing it right back to the young people. The New Testament church needed a wise, patient, strong father to teach the generations about honor.

From what I've seen, the 21st century church needs this first century teaching as well! We suffer from a lack of honor in all kinds of relationships. With a high divorce rate (almost unheard of in Paul's day) and broken homes and families, we have a whole set of problems that young Pastor Timothy knew little about! Today, many children disrespect their parents, and many parents don't value the lives of their children.

The most dangerous place for a child is not the streets of the inner city. Actually, the most dangerous place for a child today is in the womb of its own mother! As I write these words on an April day, there have been over 313,000 abortions so far this year. That means there have been 1,668 abortions today, and it's only about 1:30 in the afternoon! But the threat to children isn't just in the clinics. *USA Today* reported on April 11, 2013: "Guns kill twice as many kids as cancer does" in the United States. The Brady Campaign To Prevent Gun Violence reports 1,888 children and teens are murdered each year. The conclusion is startling: more children will be murdered in their mothers womb in a single day than will die from guns and cancer combined all year!

I'm not trying to paint mothers who have had abortions as the worst people in the world. Many of them were in very difficult situations, and they made bad decisions. The grace of God extends to all of us. I want these women to draw close to the One who loves, forgives, and accepts them, but our country simply can't turn a blind eye to the incredible number of children who never see the light of day and never have the chance to live.

I've been told the closest of all relationships is mother and child. From the smallest and most defenseless, to the greatest and strongest of us, we must confess our need for God's grace and His loving honor in all of our relationships.

There is a cry for fathers and mothers to teach another generation what honor is and how honor is demonstrated. Paul began by instructing Timothy about the honor that should be shown the elderly. "Never speak harshly to an older man, but appeal to him respectfully as though he were your own father. . . . Treat the older women as you would your mother" (1 Timothy 5:1A; 2A NLT). This instruction is a command. It demands that respect be given based on age alone. Biblical honor isn't bestowed only on those who deserve it. For instance, we are to honor our parents because "it is

My father taught me to show respect to older people because of their age. I didn't even have to know them!

right," not because they deserve it, or even because they are honorable (Ephesians 6:1b KJV).

The elderly are to be honored because of their age. Parents are to be honored because they're our mothers and fathers. Teachers, pastors, police, kings, are all to be honored because of their position alone (1 Timothy 2:1-2). It doesn't matter whether they're Democrats or Republicans! Jesus strengthened the challenge of honor when He taught, "Love your enemies, bless them that curse you, do good to them that hate you, and pray for them which despitefully use you, and persecute you." Even though the Christians in Rome were experiencing extreme persecution, Paul instructed the believers to give "honor to whom honor" is due when it came time for taxes, customs, and tribute (Romans 13:7 NIV).

HONORING PAST GENERATIONS

My father taught me to show respect to older people because of their age. I didn't even have to know them! I addressed policemen as "officer" and referred to teachers (or anyone older than me) as "Mr." or "Mrs." I was not allowed to talk back, argue, or raise my voice! It wasn't that I had to be mindless and agree with everything. My Dad would hear any opinion I had about anything—as long as I kept my voice down and watched my tone. I just had to speak with respect.

I didn't just teach my children to honor their mother and me; I showed them respect as well. Respect and honor are to be given whether they are received or not. No matter what they did or said, I refused to scream and yell at them. Whenever I disciplined them, I explained the cause and the purpose for the discipline. Then, after the discipline, I prayed with them. The only "spankable offenses" were breaking the 10 Commandments. If they lied, or stole, there would be a spanking. I didn't spank them over spilled milk. I had an accident every now and then myself!

Years ago in the first few months of our pastorate, we leased a beautiful old church. One evening, I was in the middle of an altar invitation that was going very well. The atmosphere was charged with conviction, when suddenly the huge double doors on the right side of the sanctuary burst open! My 4 year-old son Ricky entered waving his hands shouting, "Church is over, church is over, church is over!"

Suddenly, all eyes were fastened on him, and a few folks began to laugh. Then they turned their eyes toward me at the pulpit! Sensing the tension and noticing the fear in Ricky's eyes, I responded with a laugh and said: "I think Ricky's right. Church is over!" Now, when we got home, Ricky and I had a little chat about what had happened, but I didn't speak harshly to him, and there was no need for a spanking. I tried to follow Paul's admonition, "Fathers, do not exasperate your children" (Ephesians 6:4A NIV). Another version reads: "And, ye fathers, provoke not your children to wrath" (KJV). To this day, Ricky and I still laugh about that night.

When my son Rob was 18, he quit and walked off his first full time job. When I came home from the office, I gave him the old speech: "Never walk off a job until you have another one." When I finished my lecture, he said, "Dad, I know how you raised me, but for two weeks, I've been cursed at by my boss in front of the other men with language I never heard in our home. Dad, you taught me respect, and you never disrespected me like that."

I asked, "Son, did you raise your voice back at him?"

Rob replied, "Every day on the job, I treated him with respect. Dad, I held my peace."

I was so proud! Respect came "naturally" for Rob. Quite often, we don't really value respect until we endure the heartache of disrespect.

Paul gave Timothy no options: "Never speak harshly to an older man." No excuses, no justifying … just don't do it! Of course, people need correction every now and then, but when it comes to an older man, "Appeal to him respectfully, as if he were your own father." Timothy is widely believed by theologians to have been a timid young man. Even so, Paul instructed him to carefully soften his tone of voice and cautiously address older men with honor.

Many homes today have little sense of honor. Some families are a lot like Timothy's. His own father was neither Jewish nor Christian (Acts 16:1,3). No one knows the conflict this may have caused in Timothy's home, but when Paul told Timothy to "appeal to him respectfully as though he were your own father," this held special meaning to the young man. Being raised in a home with an unsaved Greek father and a Jewish Christian mother, Timothy learned to respect both!

My wife grew up in a home like Timothy's. She laughs about it today and calls it "a balanced home life." She says, "We had the balance of Daddy's cussing and Momma's praying!" Theresa's mother honored her father and taught the children to respect him, too. Theresa honored both of her parents, even though one was a Christian and the other wasn't.

Timothy's mother and grandmother must have taught him well. If they hadn't, Paul couldn't have told him to honor older men the same way he had honored his own Dad. Timothy honored his grandparents and his parents.

But parents can only impart what they've internalized. In other words, they can't give something they don't have.

From Timothy's home (and Theresa's), I realized my role as a pastor was to help all parents in our church train their children to honor others—especially their parents and the elderly. But parents can only impart what they've internalized. In other words, they can't give something they don't have.

HONOR THE NEXT GENERATION

Fathers must also show honor to the next generation. Paul told Timothy, "Talk to the younger men as you would to your own brothers … and treat the younger women with all purity as your own sisters" (1 Timothy 5:1b, 2b NLT). We must never speak down to the next generation. Paul taught Timothy to avoid dishonoring a young man by speaking to him as if he was a child. While the young men are to treat older men like fathers, fathers are to honor young men as "brothers."

I've only recently met my older brother Terry, but I've never met a more compassionate man. He reminds me so much of our father. I've already learned so much from my older brother. I love him, and he loves me. From the first moment we met, the respect and love was genuine!

My younger brother David is an amazing husband and father. He is a pharmacist, a successful professional. I had the privilege of serving as his Pastor for 29 years. He continues to serve as an elder in the church. He is my best friend, counselor, confidante, and brother in Christ. He has been a rock of support to me. He's currently writing a book entitled *The Pillar and the Pastor*. I love and respect him immensely.

I'm determined to treat young people the way I treat Terry and David. Their clothing styles may be different, and I may not understand some of their jokes, but I should never feel superior or dismiss them as irrelevant. God wants me to treat young people like a brother or sister.

Following Paul's example, I also mentored the next generation to treat younger women "with all purity as your own sisters." I have two sisters with typical Southern belle names: Patti Jo and Carol Ann. What a pair! They're the dynamic duo. Our childhood was filled with laughter and brother-sister negotiations over everything, from who was in charge when Mom and Dad were gone (that role fell to Patti Jo, a.k.a., "Little Momma") to who had the rights to the last bag of potato chips (that was usually Carol Ann who also got the first of everything!). I knew my Dad would tan my hide if I hit my sisters. The words of my father still ring in my ears: "Don't you ever hit your sister! Never, ever lay your hand on a girl! Let your sister go first! Carry your sister's books, Richard! Look out for your sisters! Don't let anything happen to your sisters!" In other words, my brother and I learned how to treat a woman. Simply put: let them be in charge, let them go first, and always let them have the last word! (Well, most of the time.) We learned to respect and honor women of all ages.

Once I was going in the Post Office and noticed a woman following closely behind, so I held the door open for her. She said angrily, "I can open my own door!" Before I thought I replied, "I'm sorry Miss. I mistook you for a lady!" If my Dad had heard me, he would have laughed out loud, and then he would have given me a spanking!

Paul also added the phrase "with all purity" to describe relationships with women. This makes perfect sense. That's the beauty of Paul's teaching on relationships in the local church. Sexual sin in the church should be revolting to us! These are our fathers and mothers, our brothers and sisters. Let's honor one another in purity.

HONOR ACROSS GENERATIONS

Today, many people have moved away from their childhood home-towns, so they connect with multiple generations only on rare occasions like holidays and family reunions. No matter how far away we may be, we can still honor people across the generations. Let me explain how I've tried to do this.

Parents

I'll tell you the truth: my Dad, Harry Robert Hilton, is my hero. During his life, I showed him the utmost respect. I never raised my hand against him. I guarded the tone of my voice, even more so when I grew up and became a man. I listened when he spoke, and I never interrupted him. I value every breakfast at Hooks Restaurant (his favorite place), prize every holiday meal together, and cherish every memory. I visit his grave and talk to him as if he can hear me. I miss him.

My mother, Anna Lee Hilton, is still living. She was "a widow indeed," even before Dad passed away. Dad's strokes and heart attacks had incapacitated him, so my incredible faithful mother cared and provided for him as best she could. When Paul taught Timothy about valuing people, he included the widow. It's the responsibility of the family to take care of aging parents when they can no longer take care of themselves. Even when Mom was still working, I made sure they had a home and provisions. Every month Theresa and I gave willingly to help them (1 Timothy 5:3-16). Today, my mother is blessed with health and continues to work. In my eyes, she is as pure as Mary, as diligent as Lydia, and as wise as Deborah. I still live to make her proud.

Pastors and elders

My wife and I have a wonderful spiritual father in Dr. B. J. Pruitt. I'm honored to be his son in the Gospel. He has been part of our life and has helped shape our destiny for decades. He continues to receive honor from us and from the churches he oversees. My sons and the leaders of the church I pastored, Calvary Church, has chosen to continue to honor him as an overseer to the church and a mentor for its leadership. Although he has never asked for it, Theresa and I have financially supported his ministry for nearly three decades (Philippians 4:15-18). We believe in him, and he believes in us. As Paul himself said, "You do not have many fathers" (1 Corinthians 4:15b KJV). Dr. Pruitt is a true father to me.

As I speak into the lives of my sons and daughters in the faith, I encourage them to create a healthy church culture of honor and respect. People in the congregation are supposed to honor their pastors and church leaders, but the spiritual fathers, the pastors and other leaders establish this culture.

Paul encouraged Timothy to be sure to bestow leaders with "double honor." According to Paul, double honor is given in two tangible ways.

First, *financial compensation.*

He wrote, "Elders who do their work well should be paid well, especially those who work hard at both preaching and teaching" (1 Timothy 5:17 NLT). In business, adequate pay helps promote a happier work environment, increased productivity, and a healthy culture. In every field, in business and the church, we invest in what we value. When we invest in someone, we honor their purpose and demonstrate their value to us (1 Timothy 5:18; Deuteronomy 25:4; Luke 10:7).

Since passing the pastorate to my successor, the church leadership has gone out of their way to honor me financially. They insisted on demonstrating honor to us in a tangible way. When I protested, they reminded me of the early years with no income, insurance, or retirement funds. They insisted on helping me prepare for the future! My successor led the way in their desire to show us "double honor." I am overwhelmed by their generosity.

Second, *trust and accountability.*

Paul wrote Timothy, "Do not listen to accusation against an elder unless it is confirmed by two or three witnesses" (1 Timothy 5:19 NLT). The atmosphere becomes toxic when gossip poisons the culture. Complaints about one another's performance, behind-the-back conversations, and envy over another's position will always result in declining morale and membership! But a culture of honor produces people who believe the best in each other and refuse to hear any rumors. It's also important to the health of a church family to allow for failure. When people can safely and confidentially confess their weakness, transparency becomes the norm, and they tend to become more accountable at home, at work, and at church. You see, when failure isn't final, we tend to open up, trust more, and accomplish far more for God's kingdom.

Be an equal opportunity dispenser of honor. Don't be a faultfinder.

Go ahead, honor everybody!

Paul's principle related to finances applies directly to the church, but trust and accountability applies in every area of life: home, work, church, clubs, teams, and friendships.

HONOR EVERYONE

Be an equal opportunity dispenser of honor. Don't be a faultfinder. Go ahead, honor everybody! You don't have to know people personally to respect them. We aren't always shown love, respect, and honor, but we should always give it. You can trust God to be the Judge of all the earth. Let's determine to "Honor all men; love the brotherhood, fear God, honor the king" (1 Peter 2:17NAS).

Paul closes his instruction to Timothy about honor with a reminder: "The sins of some are obvious, reaching the place of judgment ahead of them; the sins of others trail behind them" (1 Timothy 5:24 NIV). What a picture Paul paints! It's a scene of two men on Judgment Day. One has lived a life of unrepented sin that's already exposed. When he arrives at the Judgment, his sins are pointing a long, accusing finger at him. Another man arrives who also lived his life with unrepented sins. However, no one knew his sins. They were hidden and never exposed in his lifetime. All seems well for him as he arrives at the Judgment Seat of Christ. No sins are there waiting and pointing an accusing finger. But wait. What's that noise behind him? It's his dark, hidden sins. They have followed him into the light of God's judgment! Before Christ, hidden sins aren't hidden anymore! The writer to the Hebrews explains: "Nothing in all creation is hidden from God's sight. Everything is uncovered and laid bare before the eyes of him to whom we must give account" (Hebrews 4:13).

We don't have to worry if the sins of others are going to be revealed and judged. We can be sure God will be a just Judge! Actually, we shouldn't be concerned about exposing another person's sin anyway. Whether God exposes someone's sin in this lifetime or not is His sovereign choice. He will handle it. If we worry about anyone's sins, we should be concerned about our own—and thank Jesus that He's paid the price to completely forgive us! Instead of pointing fingers, let's be sure to honor, love, and respect one another as a family in Christ. Let's establish a culture of honor toward our fathers, mothers, brothers and sisters in the Lord.

An atmosphere of honor creates a healthy and safe environment where people can thrive. Whether it's in a local church, a business, or a family, honor pleases God, and God blesses the people who give honor!

CHAPTER ELEVEN

GENEROSITY

"Tell those who are rich in this world not to be proud and not to trust in their money, which will soon be gone. But their trust should be in the living God, who richly gives us all we need for our enjoyment. Tell them to use their money to do good. They should be rich in good works and should give generously, always being ready to share with others what God has given them. By doing this they will be storing up their treasure as a good foundation for the future so that they may take hold of real life" (1 Timothy 6:17-19 NLT).

P aul was nearing the end of his letter to Timothy when he turned his focus to the marketplace, money, and ministry. In recent years, reports of financial mismanagement have plagued Christianity. The greed of a few has cast a shadow over the generosity of the many. A small number have merchandised the anointing, but God has turned this for good because the desire for integrity has inspired many churches to a greater level of genuine accountability.

Individuals, couples, families, and churches are called to be generous with all God has given them. It's one of the most vivid ways we shine as lights to a darkened world.

When we planted Calvary Church 29 years ago, we formed four levels of accountability. I trusted myself, but I wanted to remove any cause for suspicion and provide a safe environment for those who came to our church. First, we created the Financial Accountability Council, called the "FACS," which met monthly to examine the books and make budget recommendations. Second, the FACS sent their report to the board of elders for decisions. Third, an outside church and clergy accounting firm audited each month's receipts. And last, an outside group of ministers that we called "the presbytery" received annual financial reports and met with our leaders to ask hard questions about me: as a man, my ministry, and my marriage.

Some people thought this level of accountability was unnecessary, but we continued that practice, and God blessed it. My desire as a father has been to be an example of integrity and to teach the necessity of financial purity to my congregation and to my children in the faith.

THE MARKETPLACE

The key to the right perspective about money is generosity! Paul began his final thoughts by encouraging honesty and respect on the job. He wrote, "If your master is a Christian, that is no excuse for being disrespectful. You should work all the harder" (1 Timothy 6:2A NLT).

Slavery was a sad fact of life in the Apostle Paul's time. It is estimated that 25 percent of the population of the Roman Empire were slaves. Among them was a growing number of Christian converts. Most of these Christian slaves had unbelieving masters, but some had Christian masters. When both master and slave got saved, it really shook up slavery! They became brothers and sisters in Christ. When it was believed and practiced, Christianity brought about the death of slavery. Paul was known to ask personally for the freedom of the slave (Philemon 9-19).

The marketplace is different in the 21st century, but many employees still feel like slaves. Some Christians are still "under the yoke" (verse 1). Everyday, they go to a job they hate to perform a task they despise. When asked why they do it, they respond, "For the money." Their sole motive to get up and go to work is money. While their employer isn't their master, money is!

Some employers are unfair to their employees, taking advantage of them. James, the brother of Jesus, and Paul rebuke this abuse (see Colossians 3: 22-3:1 and James 5:1-4). The abusive employer is a slave to money as well. When he's asked why he pays poorly he responds, "For the money." In this, the unjust employer and the enslaved employee have the same misplaced goal. Both are slaves to a master named "money."

THE KEY OF GENEROSITY

God calls all Christians to break the yoke of being enslaved to money! How? The key to unlocking the shackles of slavery to money is *generosity*. We work so that we can give. We prosper so that we can give. We're blessed to be a blessing. As an employee, work to give. As an employer, be fair and kind to your employees. Generosity, though, begins at home. Let me outline some principles of generosity parents can impart to their children.

First, *work to give honor to the real boss, the true Master.*

We work hard and give it our best effort "so that the name of God and his teaching will not be shamed" (1 Timothy 6:1B NLT). Being successful and prosperous in our career is much more fulfilling when we give the glory to God. "Work with enthusiasm, as though you were working for the Lord rather than for people" (Ephesians 6:7 NLT). Generosity will make you the boss and your job your employee! Your career should be your servant. It exists to help you be a witness. In humility

We work so that we can give.

We prosper so that we can give.

We're blessed to be a blessing.

recognize that God gave you the job, the business, your talents, or the career so that you might serve and honor Him in it.

As an employer, your motive should be to prosper so that you might give even more. Begin by being generous with your employees. "Remember that the Lord will reward each one of us for the good we do, whether we are slaves or free. And in the same way, you masters must treat your slaves right . . . you both have the same Master in Heaven, and he has no favorites" (Ephesians 6:8-9).

This is an important principle for Pastors and church leaders to remember as well. You are servants of God's people, and He loves them as much as He loves you. Don't get wrapped up in the recognition men give. You are a servant of the Lord, so give generously of your time, talent, and treasure to be a blessing to God's people.

Second, *work to give generously and meet the needs of others.*

In order to be generous, we must not be greedy for possessions. As a matter of fact, when we give generously with joy, God will make sure that we have an abundance so that we can give again and again. Paul reminds us, "You will be enriched in every way so that you can be generous on every occasion" (2 Corinthians 9:11a NIV). Jesus taught that people are more important than things, and relationships are more important than money! When two brothers came to him arguing over an inheritance, their love for one another was dying as they fought over possessions, Jesus warned them, "Beware! Don't be greedy for what you don't have." Then He reminded them, "Life is not measured by how much you own" (Luke 12:15b NLT). As the crowd listened, Jesus warned them against hoarding. He reminded them of the importance of our relationship with God and the certainty that we take nothing with us when we die (Luke 12:16-21). "It's more blessed to give than to receive." Be generous. It's the way God's kingdom works.

Third, *work to leave a legacy.*

Paul taught the next generation: "Godliness with contentment is great gain. For we brought nothing into the world and we can take nothing out of it" (1 Timothy 6:6-7 NIV). Teach young people to be a generous generation. Contentment is a fleeting thing. The more we have the more we want, and the more we want the more we think we need! Paul challenged the next generation to hold things loosely—to live with an open hand. "Command them to do good, to be rich in good deeds, and to be generous and willing to share" (1 Timothy 6:18 NIV).

My son Rob illustrated this principle in a recent sermon. He had a large jar filled with dimes. He brought his daughter Chloe on the stage and asked her to catch some dimes in her hands as he tipped the jar over. Rob began to pour the dimes into her hands. As they began to fall out of her hands to the floor, she closed her hands to hold on to the few dimes her hands could hold. Then Rob stopped pouring them out on her closed hands. When Chloe realized her father had stopped, she again opened her hands, and Rob began to pour them out again. As the dimes continued falling into her open hands and cascading down to the floor, we were reminded that God gives a continuous overflow to open hands!

Like Chloe, we must learn that we don't need more than our hands can hold. God gives the overflow so that we can be a blessing to others in need. Teach the next generation contentment, and they'll learn this valuable priority: "People before things!"

Theresa and I served as evangelists before we planted Calvary Church. For several years, we traveled to youth revivals, conferences, and camps. Many people helped us during those years. I'll always be grateful for the generosity of Ron and Christi Bishop. Even though they were missionaries, they took the time to call their friends who pastored churches to fill our itinerary with six months of new doors of ministry. Dr. B.J. Pruitt and Pastor Joe Ratliff promoted our young ministry. Rev. John Cook at International Bible College in San Antonio, Texas, let us use a motor home during our last 18 months as evangelists. Pastor Ralph and Marquita Baker provided new clothes for my children for a couple of years! These wonderful people sacrificed and invested into my family. They will share in the heavenly reward for all that my wife, my children and I will ever accomplish.

You see, we gave and God gave back to us—abundantly! Recently, Theresa and I were reminiscing about some of those evangelistic meetings and rejoicing in the memories of so many salvations. Suddenly, it dawned on us that we had lived out of our car during most of those years before God provided us with a motor home. We laughed out loud at the thought that we had been homeless and didn't even know it. We were giving of ourselves to see people come to Christ—and it was no sacrifice in the least. We attended many missions conferences and left having emptied our pockets for missionaries. The joy and fulfillment of generosity made those days some of the best years of our lives!

Be certain to pass on the joy that generosity gives to life. Only by giving generously to those in need can we "take hold of the life that is truly life" (1 Timothy 6:19C NIV).

Often, we traveled for hours hoping to receive a meal at the next church or youth camp. Mark Holcomb was only 13 or 14 years old when he accompanied us from Elkton, Maryland to Williamsport, Pennsylvania. He tells the story of our stop at a fast food restaurant and how we searched in and under the seats for enough change to pay for a couple of Happy Meals! At the youth camp that year, he came forward to give his life to the call of Christ. Mark is now president of Awakening Ministries, and together with his wife Debbie, he travels around the world sharing the Gospel message. When you give your all to meet the needs of others and for the cause of Christ, your giving will inspire others to give generously.

Contentment and obedience to God's will enable us to leave a powerful legacy of generosity for the next generation. A selfish person never spends the time or the money to invest in the next generation. This attitude was well expressed in a bumper sticker I saw on the back of a motor home the other day: "I'm spending my grandchildren's inheritance!" Whatever you've got to do, break away from living for yourself. Make the sacrifice, make it often, and make it joyfully.

God thinks generationally. He doesn't focus on today. He's the God of Abraham, Isaac, and Jacob. Your giving, of tithes and every kind of offering, will set an example for your children which will produce a harvest for generations to come. The writer of Hebrews tells us that when Abraham tithed, his great grandson Levi "paid tithes in Abraham. For he was yet in the loins of his father, when Melchisedec met him" (Hebrews 7:9-10 KJV). For the generous, there are blessings in your DNA. I have a grandson named Levi. I like this promise!

I have six grandsons and four granddaughters. It thrills me to think that Chloe, Judah, Aaliyah, Oliver, Andrew, Addison, Levi, Colin, Ava, and Ryan have already tithed through my giving! You're winning battles your children won't have to fight. Each generation stands on the shoulders of their fathers. If we live unselfishly, our children can begin where we end. They can start where we finished— with more resources, more faith, and more victory. Hallelujah!!

Begin now to plan for the next generation. Invest in them, pour into them, and when it is time, let them have the reigns. Leave a legacy of faith, prayer, worship and fellowship, godliness, honor, and generosity.

CHAPTER TWELVE

TRANSITION AND SUCCESSION

"As the Lord commanded his servant Moses, so Moses commanded Joshua, and Joshua did it; he left nothing undone of all that the Lord commanded Moses" (Joshua 11:15 KJV).

The goal of parenting natural or spiritual children is to impart life, faith, and purpose to them. Some parents start this process with good intentions, but they have a hard time letting their children take responsibility for their own lives. It's important to be aware of the stages of transition and succession—in a family and in the family of God. Recently, I've had some new experiences with this process.

The year 2014 marks my 40th year of ministry. I successfully transitioned my pastorate on October 18th, 2013. Let me share with you some of the emotions that my wife and I have felt—and continue to feel.

First, let me say, it's going great! Theresa and I are rejoicing in the continued growth of the church we planted 29 years ago. Calvary Church is thriving, already adding additional Sunday services to help facilitate the growth. My successor is dynamic and a true shepherd!

Our new life in Christ's plan consists of consulting pastors and churches. We also are thrilled to be touching the mission field in person more frequently than I ever would have had time for as Senior Pastor. In addition, God has faithfully kept me busy as a conference speaker. Theresa is busy writing and recording a new worship album, as well as keeping speaking engagements.

TRANSITION IS LETTING GO

The transition phase is full of changes—and as always, change is, well, "scary exciting!" I'm adjusting emotionally. I loved pastoring. I didn't resign as a pastor; I willingly passed the baton. My heart has always been to elevate others. My destiny is to push, train, develop, and motivate my children and other young people to fulfill their destiny. I love the next generation! No, I didn't pass the baton because I was done. Far from it. I did it willingly in obedience to God. I followed the biblical examples: Moses and Joshua, Elijah and Elisha, Paul and Timothy, and Jesus and the 120 in the Upper Room. I knew God wasn't finished with me. I wasn't leaving His harvest field. I would just be laboring for the Lord in a new and wider portion of His field.

Emotionally, the nearest comparison is when my daughter Rebecca was married. Rebecca is my baby girl. I truly spoiled her and continue to do so! As the ceremony began, we stood together in the hall just behind the double doors of the sanctuary. The rest of the wedding party had already reached the front. The music was about to change to signal the bride's entrance, when I turned to her and made an offer: "If you'll call this off, I'll buy you a new Mustang!"

She smiled and said, "Daddy, I love Jesse."

I grinned, "I know. It's just hard to let my little girl go." We embraced, walked down the aisle, I gave her away—and everything changed.

After the wedding, powerful emotions flooded Theresa and me when we came back to the empty house. Finally, one morning, after a few days of awkward silence, I walked up to Theresa in the kitchen and reached out my hand to shake hers. I said, "Hi, my name is Richard. What's yours? You look familiar!" We laughed and slow danced all around the kitchen. Together, we had raised a family and built a church and other ministries. What a wonderful opportunity to get to know the love of my life again!

Transitioning the pastorate was a little like giving away my daughter's hand in marriage. It was a life-changing event, and it was beautiful, but it came at a cost. The ceremony, the photographer, the reception, the future ... it was a new day for everyone.

Transition is a good thing, but it requires change. Successful succession requires "letting go." You must let the next generation lead. Like any good Dad, my role has changed in my daughter's life. I'm now her husband Jesse's biggest fan. I'm available if Jesse and Rebecca need me, but Jesse is her husband—her main man. That's not my role any longer. The success of their marriage requires the absence of "in-law" interference! (Can somebody say, "Amen!")

> It was a life-changing event, and it was beautiful, but it came at a cost.

Rob and his wife Monica are the new pastors. Again, that's not my role any longer. The success of the new shepherd requires the absence of "previous pastor" interference! (I'm sure Rob would say, "Amen!" to that.) However, I can be valuable to Rob in counsel, prayer, and loyal support. My role has changed. I'm now Rob's biggest fan. I'm lifting up the hands of my new shepherd! Rob has already scheduled me to return to fill the pulpit for him on occasion. I've honored him, he knows his leadership is safe, and he insists on honoring me.

TRANSITION IS TAKING THE FUTURE BY THE THROAT

Transition can be the most God-honoring thing people can see us accomplish. Our entire Tri-Cities region has witnessed the change. Our mayor, the congressman's aide, and our state senator came to the transition ceremony, and they stayed through the entire 75-minute service. We made the focus our new pastors. We celebrated the future, rather than becoming melancholy over the past.

Dr. Samuel R. Chand, Bishop B. Courtney McBath, Bishop Brian C. Greene, Dr. B.J. Pruitt, and Pastor Don Shilts conducted the charges. I will always be grateful to them. The only part I played in the ceremony was at the very end when I removed a Jewish Prayer Shawl (representing the pastoral mantle) and placed it on Rob's shoulders. I then gave him the Bible I'd preached from for years, knelt before him and prayed. Finally, I introduced him and his wife to the congregation and brought his children to the platform to a rousing standing ovation!

Calvary Church is moving forward. Our new Pastor began to cast vision immediately with a series entitled: "This Is Who We Are!" The elders and church leaders have really taken hold of the vision. I'm so proud of them! There have also been some physical changes to the facilities to make them more, well, "next generation." We didn't need many because I asked Rob to begin making changes he would like over the last three years of my pastorate. We made these changes as part of the Transition Plan, so that as changes were made, people said, "It must be okay. Pastor Richard wants it done." This way, we didn't put Rob in the position of having to make so many changes as soon as I was gone, and this made the bigger changes happen more gradually. Plus, I have to admit it: I really like change! People are being saved every Sunday! It's epic!

Theresa and I are also moving forward. Years ago, my first pastor used to say he was never retiring, but he would occasionally experience a "refiring." I think I now know what he meant. This certainly isn't retirement! In speaking, consulting, missions, and other pursuits, Theresa and I are working harder than ever. I'm just wearing a different hat ... and I'm loving it!

Will you follow me as I follow Christ in raising a new generation of young people to know, love, and serve Jesus Christ? Many of those who have come to the end of this book are fathers and mothers who long to leave a legacy of faith in the lives of their children. Some are mothers and grandmothers, like Lois and Eunice, who are having a dramatic impact on young lives. And others are leaders in the church who, like Paul, are investing their hearts, their time, and their gifts in young men and women who will become tomorrow's leaders.

Will you follow me as I follow Christ in raising a new generation of young people to know, love, and serve Jesus Christ?

I appreciate your heart for the Lord and for the young people you love. As you love and lead, you face obstacles. No matter how steep the mountain, don't stop climbing. No matter how deep the ocean, keep swimming. Young people desperately need your love, your support, and your leadership. You're doing a great job, but excel still more!

A RESOURCE

...for you, for your leadership team, and for your church

In his years in pastoral ministry, Dr. Richard Hilton has been involved in the full range of leadership: from helping pastors and their leadership teams determine God's direction for their churches . . . to caring for those who are struggling. Many different organizations use Dr. Hilton's insights and expertise in the areas of coaching, counseling, and consulting.

Dr. Hilton describes these roles:

Coaching

From time to time, even the most successful leaders need a fresh injection of inspiration, fresh ideas, and direction for strategic planning. In athletics, business, and ministry, coaches play a vital role in helping people achieve their God-given potential. And sometimes, a seasoned coach can make all the difference in a person's future. My passion is to coach people—whether they're parents, professionals, or pastors—so they'll be ready for the game-changing moments in their lives.

Counseling

Leadership requires a blend of strength and compassion. Many leaders give and serve so much that they run dry emotionally, physically, and spiritually. In addition, they're not immune from the normal stresses and disappointments everyone else endures. From their family and marriage to their finances and friendships, crushing stress is very real in the lives of leaders! As a Board Certified Pastoral Counselor, God has given me a heart to use 40 years of ministry and 37 years of marriage to help lift the burdens and strengthen the hearts of leaders, their families, and their teams. Every leader needs someone whose counsel is biblical and whose confidentiality they can trust.

Consulting

Building a united and cohesive leadership team, casting and implementing an ever-increasing vision, promoting a healthy culture of progressive growth, and gaining and maintaining momentum are necessary components for success. Getting from where we are to where we desire to go requires a heart humble enough to seek advice. My goal is to provide the "how to's" for the journey for pastors, business leaders, and their teams.

For more information about these opportunities...
Email: erica@visitcalvary.com
Or online: www.hfmrevival.com

Richard Hilton is well-read and very astute in helping Pastors in their personal and professional lives. If you need a voice of wisdom, if you need godly counsel, if you need an experienced leader, look no further. Contact Bishop Richard Hilton today.

—Dr. Samuel R. Chand, Leadership Consultant and author
of *Cracking Your Church's Culture Code* (www.samchand.com)

TO ORDER MORE COPIES

GENERATION

to

GENERATION

Developing *faithful* young leaders
in the home & *church*

Richard L. Hilton

To order more copies, go to
http://www.hiltonfamilyministries.com.

CPSIA information can be obtained
at www.ICGtesting.com
Printed in the USA
JSHW030330020322
23496JS00005B/21